"Feng shui has totally changed the feel of my classroom. I, along with my students, do not feel overwhelmed. We have noticed that the atmosphere is a very positive one. Thanks to Kristina Hollinger for showing me a new way of bringing positive energy into both my classroom and home. Awesome!"

-Julie Jasinski
5th Grade Teacher
Cicero School District 99

"Kristina is focused on improving the lives of those around her by working to continually apply best practices to student learning and to instruction. She works collaboratively with others and seeks to develop meaningful partnerships within the school and the community."

-Dr. Sandra Niemiera
Clinical Faculty, Department of Leadership
Concordia University, River Forest, IL

Teaching from the Heart with Feng Shui

Inspired Living for Teachers, Parents, and Kids

KRISTINA HOLLINGER

BALBOA
PRESS
A DIVISION OF HAY HOUSE

Copyright © 2017 Kristina Hollinger.

All rights reserved. No part of this book may be used or reproduced by any means, graphic, electronic, or mechanical, including photocopying, recording, taping or by any information storage retrieval system without the written permission of the author except in the case of brief quotations embodied in critical articles and reviews.

This book is a work of non-fiction. Unless otherwise noted, the author and the publisher make no explicit guarantees as to the accuracy of the information contained in this book and in some cases, names of people and places have been altered to protect their privacy.

Balboa Press books may be ordered through booksellers or by contacting:

Balboa Press
A Division of Hay House
1663 Liberty Drive
Bloomington, IN 47403
www.balboapress.com
1 (877) 407-4847

Because of the dynamic nature of the Internet, any web addresses or links contained in this book may have changed since publication and may no longer be valid. The views expressed in this work are solely those of the author and do not necessarily reflect the views of the publisher, and the publisher hereby disclaims any responsibility for them.

The author of this book does not dispense medical advice or prescribe the use of any technique as a form of treatment for physical, emotional, or medical problems without the advice of a physician, either directly or indirectly. The intent of the author is only to offer information of a general nature to help you in your quest for emotional and spiritual well-being. In the event you use any of the information in this book for yourself, which is your constitutional right, the author and the publisher assume no responsibility for your actions.

Any people depicted in stock imagery provided by Thinkstock are models, and such images are being used for illustrative purposes only.
Certain stock imagery © Thinkstock.

Print information available on the last page.

ISBN: 978-1-5043-8216-8 (sc)
ISBN: 978-1-5043-8217-5 (e)

Library of Congress Control Number: 2017909412

Balboa Press rev. date: 06/20/2017

Table of Contents

Acknowledgments...ix
Foreword...xi
Introduction...xiii

Part I: Feng Shui Basics

Chapter 1: Fundamentals of Feng Shui ♥ 1
Origin of Feng Shui, Flow of Chi, Yin and Yang, Introduction to the Bagua Map and the Five Elements

Chapter 2: Cleaning with a Twist ♥ 11
How to Clean and Declutter with Intention

Chapter 3: Applying Elemental Cures with Décor ♥ 16
The Five Elements, Constructive and Destructive Cycles

Chapter 4: Setting Your Intention for Manifestation ♥ 25
How to Seal with Intention, Change Your Thoughts and Change Your Life

Part II: Feng Shui in the Classroom

Chapter 5: The Research Supporting Feng Shui in Schools.......33
Chapter 6: Creating Flow in Your Classroom ♥ 42
Furniture Placement and Cleaning Routines

Chapter 7: Applying the Elements to the Classroom ♥ 53
Using the Bagua Map to Support the Energy of Your Classroom

v

**Chapter 8: Positive Self-Talk and Mindfulness in the
                 Classroom**♥ 60
*Raise the Energetic Vibration of Your Students and Your
Classroom with Positive Self-Talk and Breathing Techniques*

Part III: Feng Shui Your Home

Chapter 9: Creating a Sanctuary 69
Chapter 10: The Main Entrance 72
Chapter 11: The Master Bedroom♥ 78
Chapter 12: The Kitchen 86
Chapter 13: Uplifting the Bathrooms 92
Chapter 14: Feng Shui for Kids♥ 96
Chapter 15: Enjoying Your Feng Shui Home 101

Part IV: Personalized Feng Shui

Chapter 16: Birth Elements and How They Interact♥ 105
Chapter 17: Discover Your Personal Direction♥ 112
**Chapter 18: Attracting Abundance with Transcendental
                 Cures**♥..**117**
Chapter 19: Finding Balance by Aligning with Nature 125
Chapter 20: Finding Balance Within 128
Chapter 21: Finding Your Flow♥ 131

Appendix: Nine Do-It-Yourself Feng Shui Activities!

♥All chapters with a heart symbol correspond to an activity in the appendix.

1. The Nine Areas of Life: Using the Bagua Map
2. Let's Get Energized: Understanding the Flow of Chi
3. Improve Your Life with the Elements: Introduction to the Five Elements
4. All About Affirmations
5. Let's Find More Balance: Yin & Yang

6. Feng Shui Your Bedroom
7. All About You: Finding Your Best Direction
8. Fun with Feng Shui Numbers
9. Living the Feng Shui Way: Evaluate Your Personal Chi

References 161

Acknowledgments

This book is the product of so many great influences. First and foremost, I want to thank my husband Andy for allowing me to extend my work into the evening hours so that I could spread the empowering message of feng shui. I am also deeply grateful to my daughter, Abby, who was only two when I wrote this. She made sure the process would not consume me and kept me motivated every step of the way. To my parents, thank you for your support throughout the years. You have taught me that there are no limits to what you can do!

Throughout this process, there have been so many helpful professionals who have assisted me along the way. Thank you to Harley Richardson for editing my very first book. I honor your ambition and commitment, and I know you will do great things throughout your career! A huge thank you to Shuling Yong. I am so grateful that it was our destiny to work together. You made this book come to life with such a powerful video! Julie Armstrong, you always take the best professional pictures. Your friendship and support throughout the years has been such a gift!

Thank you to Julie Jasinski and Katie Hedrich. They were the first educators and administrators who allowed me into their classroom and office so that I could give them a feng shui consultation. Thank you for opening your hearts and minds. Education is better because of professionals like you. I hope you're experiencing magical results!

It is with deep gratitude that I thank the Hay House team, especially founder Louise Hay and CEO Reid Tracy. It is because of the Hay House Writer's Workshop that I found the courage, confidence, and motivation to write this book and share my message with the world. Balboa Press, thank you for giving new writers like me a chance to share our light. Cheryl Grace, author of *Feng Shui Simply: Change Your Life from the Inside Out,* thank you so much for taking the time to review the manuscript and provide me with honest, expert feedback. Other Hay House authors who inspired me indirectly are Doreen Virtue Ph.D. and Dr. Wayne Dyer. I cannot thank them enough. They teach from their hearts and have greatly influenced me with this book!

And last, but certainly not least, thank you Laurie Pawli. When you founded the Feng Shui School of Chicago you probably could not have predicted the impact you would have on people's lives. Well, you completely transformed mine! I am so grateful for all your wisdom. Professor Thomas Lin Yun and your mom would be *very* proud of you!

Foreword

Teaching from the Heart with Feng Shui is a must-read for teachers everywhere, not to mention the entire adult population. *Teaching from the Heart with Feng Shui* expresses the unique perspective of Certified Feng Shui Consultant and elementary school instructor, Kristina Hollinger, as she shares her views on feng shui for the classroom. Along with her recommendations that can be easily implemented, her theories are backed up with factual documentation to create a supportive environment for students and teachers.

This enlightening book, which teaches you how to bring energy into various spaces, goes beyond the classroom, and connects with the energy of your heart. You will begin to *feel* a new energy starting to emerge as you connect with this book. You will be inspired with a new insight to help children learn in a more intentional way.

You will learn how to place the bagua (the 9 square grid) in a classroom; you will learn the best colors to use; how to use various shapes; and how the five elements (water, wood, fire, earth, metal) can bring about the perfect vibrational energy in the classroom. As you become acquainted with feng shui (pronounced *feng schway*), you will become more aware of how our environment impacts our thoughts, our feelings, and our success in life.

During Kristina's certification process at The Feng Shui School of Chicago, her path was always clear, concise, and organized. Her questions were always thoughtful and tactful. As a feng shui instructor, I can sense the ability and intention of my students. Kristina possesses the natural ability to assess a space and recommend the appropriate feng shui adjustments for the best results. She is one of the most talented I have known.

As the Founder and Director of the Feng Shui School of Chicago, Kristina and I joined together in great discussions about feng shui. As we discussed feng shui solutions, I shared the story of my own path of feng shui with her. Beginning in my teens, my design style was to create balanced spaces. It didn't occur to me until many years later, that my "gut" was feeling the feng shui influence to create flowing energy as my mind automatically rearranged each room that I walked into. All of the years that my parents watched me as I painted various colors on my bedroom walls, made window treatments, studied Design at Northern Illinois University, and worked at Chicago's Merchandise Mart... it all came full circle in 2001 and made sense when I learned about feng shui and began my study with Professor Thomas Lin Yun. It was my passion!

Kristina Hollinger shares that same passion for feng shui. You will feel her passion as you read each informative chapter of *Teaching from the Heart with Feng Shui*. Her book will inspire instructors to see their spaces with a new, fresh mindset that will be transferred into the hearts of their students through the love of feng shui.

Laurie Pawli

Feng Shui School of Chicago, Founder and Director

Introduction

"Yesterday I was clever, so I wanted to change the world. Today I am wise, so I am changing myself."
-Rumi

There I was, newly married and living in the city. I had a new teaching job and a workout regimen that kept me busy. My husband and I had finally emerged from the credit card debt that accumulated from planning a downtown wedding. So I guess things were starting to look up. Maybe it was the post-wedding blues (supposedly that's "a thing"), but I still felt like something was missing and longed for something more. From the outside things seemed to be going pretty good, so what was wrong?

As I looked around our Chicago South Loop apartment, I had an uneasy feeling. All the walls were stark white and hadn't been painted since we moved in three years ago. In my spare time, I decided I would start to spruce up the place; make it a little more welcoming and comfortable. That's when I discovered feng shui.

I learned how to arrange furniture and decorate with specific shapes and colors so that our home looked *and* felt better. Our apartment finally felt more inviting, and the months following the feng shui enhancements were a total whirlwind!

My husband and I found out we were expecting our first baby, and he had gotten an exciting advancement in his career. I started to feel less uneasy and more fulfilled in my day-to-day life. More importantly, that new-calm was transferred to my second home, my classroom. I quickly learned that when you create a flow of consistency between your personal and professional life, you can breathe easier. Life just feels lighter!

This knowledge was all too good to keep to myself, so I earned a Feng Shui Consultant Certification through the Feng Shui School of Chicago with Laurie Pawli, a former student of the late Professor Thomas Lin Yun. I became a Red Ribbon Professional Member of the International Feng Shui Guild in 2016. Although I knew I wanted to help others heal their lives with feng shui as a consultant, my heart told me I needed to do something *even more.*

I knew from experience that teachers and parents have the most *selfless* jobs in the world, and yet it is a necessary to make time for yourself in order to give the best care to others. I wanted to help teachers and parents create more balance and joy in their daily lives. So, I started this book…

What is Teaching from the Heart?

Teaching from the heart is showing up as your best self. It is feeling inner peace, even when chaos abounds.

Children will do as you do, not as you say. When adults make self-care a priority, they feel better and more vibrant. They are able to set a more positive example for children.

Teachers and parents can nurture their personal energy by creating more balanced living and working environments. As a result, they will have more of themselves to give without feeling depleted. This book offers feng shui methods to preserve your individual energy, as well as ways to support children's energy, so that everyone can live in harmony and go with the flow of life, versus swimming against the current.

Why feng shui?

Feng shui is a tangible way that you can minimize your problems or frustrations. When something in your life feels uneasy, you can address it head-on in a physical way instead of stewing over it in your mind. Feng shui allows you to visually see your environment change, which in turn gives you greater peace and hope for your future.

Living in the flow with feng shui is about being present. It is about knowing that *you have the power to attract the life you desire.* You were born to dream big and live big. All of your desires were given divinely to you because you were meant to use your gifts and make this world a better place. Feng shui is a method that can help you live a more purposeful life and mold your dreams into reality.

When you embrace the present moment, you are truly alive and experiencing life as it is meant to be. Feng shui is just one way to help you become more mindful in your day-to-day life. It is an avenue that can connect you to Heaven while you are here on Earth. It links your inner and outer worlds, so that your true self is reflected in all that you do. It helps you connect your personal life to your professional life so that you feel a greater sense of well-being and fluidity throughout your days.

As you go through this life journey, you have lessons to learn. There will be challenges, and unfortunately, feng shui cannot change that. What feng shui *can* do is become a tool to help you through all of life's seasons. Feng shui gives you a new perspective on how to deal with situations in your home or classroom, and it empowers you to change your course and attract what you truly want.

How to Use this Book

In order to teach from the heart, you must first go within yourself. **Part I** will provide you with the basics of feng shui and ask you to think about your personal life. Which areas of your life are you feeling empowered? Where do you seek improvements? When you make improvements to your personal life, you will start to see the positive effects trickle into your professional life.

Part II provides suggestions on how to implement your feng shui practice in the classroom. It gives teachers and students opportunities to play active roles in creating a more uplifting, productive classroom environment on a daily basis. If you choose, you may teach the strategies to your students or your own children. Just as teaching children yoga and meditation gives them coping skills they can use for the rest of their lives, feng shui is another pathway to the enlightenment of our youth.

Part III invites you to bring the harmony home! You will learn how to apply feng shui to the four most important areas of the house, and there is a special section geared towards kids' rooms too!

The last part of this book helps you personalize your feng shui practice. In **Part IV** you will learn your personal birth element and your "best directions." You will get a better understanding of the personal energy of your family members and students so that you can make feng shui adjustments that support everyone's energy to the fullest potential. Most importantly, this section gives you daily self-care techniques that will keep you feeling more grounded and less frazzled in your day-to-day activities.

There are nine activities which can be found in the appendix. These will help you apply the feng shui concepts to your home and classroom with greater ease and clarity. The activities are best matched to specific chapters of the book, but they can be practiced at any time, in any order.

These nine activities are for teachers, parents, students and all learners of feng shui. Try them for yourself, and then share the feng shui strategies with children at your leisure. The activities will provide kids with a foundation to become more aware of their surroundings and take ownership of their environment. Regardless of how the activities are used, they will empower children and adults alike.

Three things to remember when using feng shui to get the results you desire:

- **Feng Shui is meant to be fun!** Many of the concepts are simple. Don't stress over "doing it right." You can get creative and make your space reflect your own personal style and preferences. Let your intuition guide you. You will know if an adjustment you make feels right or not. As long your heart is in the right place, things will work out for you. When I started feng shui I based all my knowledge from the internet. My environment looked better and things started to shift in my life because of the *intentional* design and decor choices.
- **Try to minimize the adjustments.** The knowledge of feng shui can be very exciting and empowering! It's easy to want to apply it all at once. However, it is best to focus on one room at a time or try a couple of changes around the house before completely changing everything. If you make too many enhancements at once you may not know what was effective or ineffective for you.
- **As you make changes to your space, remember that everything happens in perfect timing.** Although we want our desires to manifest right away, sometimes there is something even better in store for you. Trust in Divine, perfect timing. What you need is on its way!

You are about to expand into an even better, brighter version of yourself. By tending to your environment, you will find great healing within. When you heal yourself, you impact those around you. Let us move on from trying to change the world, and into the great wisdom of changing ourselves.

Part I
Feng Shui Basics

Chapter 1
Fundamentals of Feng Shui

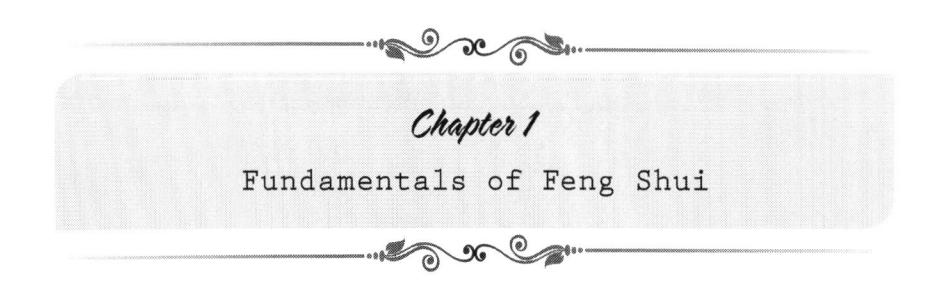

"When the student is ready, the teacher will appear."
-Chinese Proverb

Always Know Why

As a consultant it is not only my responsibility to give you the best personalized advice possible, but to also explain *why* I am giving you these suggestions. You are about to be introduced to the basics of feng shui so that you have a general understanding of the practice. You will learn that although there are different schools of feng shui, they all share the same basic fundamental truths in regards to *chi* (also spelled *qi*), *yin and yang, the bagua map*, and *the five elements*. Once you are introduced to these concepts, you will have a deeper understanding of why the feng shui suggestions throughout this book will work for you!

What exactly is feng shui?

Feng shui (pronounced feng schway), is an ancient Chinese practice that has been passed down for over 3,000 years. The words *feng shui* translate to "wind" and "water." Together the words represent harmony and balance. The ancient art is based on the flow of "chi," or the energy that makes up all things. Chi can flow fast or slow, and it has an impact on our daily lives. Feng shui is related to subjects of nature such as physics and astrology, but it is *not* affiliated with any religion.

By making adjustments to your environment, it is believed that you can make a positive impact on your health, finances and more. If there is an area of your life you wish to improve, you can make adjustments to your home, car, or office. By creating a more harmonious living or working environment, not only will they look and feel better, but you will start to see improvements in different areas of your life. Don't believe me? You will soon try it for yourself, and see how it can work for you!

Form School

The Form School is the original version of feng shui. The people of ancient China studied the land and learned the best placement for their homes and farms in order to yield the most plentiful harvest. We learned about the flow of chi and the balance of yin and yang from the Form School.

Some of the teachings from Form School are still applicable today. For example, modern schools of feng shui still acknowledge that it is best to have a mountain behind your home. Even if you do not live in the mountains, tall trees or a hill behind your home could create a "mountain," providing you with a greater sense of security.

Compass Feng Shui

Some people will refer to Compass Schools as the traditional method. Compass Schools use the compass directions and various feng shui calculations to determine which areas of the home are associated with specific areas of life, such as health, wealth and relationships.

Within the Compass Schools, the Flying Star Feng Shui is considered one of the most powerful methods. It takes into consideration specific information about a site. For example, it takes into consideration the birth dates of residents in conjunction with the

Flying Star to help identify the relationship between them and the energy pattern of their environment.

Western Feng Shui

The Compass School can be more complex, which is why other branches of feng shui have been developed. Schools such as the Black Sect (BTB) and Intuitive Modern Feng Shui are more practical to apply in the contemporary western world.

Professor Thomas Lin Yun brought the BTB School of Feng Shui to the United States in the 1980s. This modern version uses the front door entrance as a point of reference to enhance the environment, versus other traditional schools, which use the compass directions to make adjustments. His methods made feng shui relatable and accessible to the Western culture. Professor Lin Yun's definition of feng shui is as follows:

> **"Feng Shui is the method that people naturally use to choose and locate, build and construct, or adapt and change their working and living environments for maximum health, wealth, and well-being according to the knowledge then available."**

According to this definition, as you start to try feng shui, remember to do the best you can with the knowledge you have at the time. As you learn more about the topic, you will be able to make adjustments that serve you better as time goes on.

The International Feng Shui Guild (IFSG) is a group that is comprised of feng shui masters and practitioners from all different backgrounds: Form School, Compass Feng Shui, and Western Feng Shui. Although each school has variations, each one is beneficial when you set your intention for the results you wish to achieve.

What is chi?

You are about to learn how to make cures, or adjustments, to your environment in a conscious effort to improve the flow of chi (also written as *qi*). Chi is how the ancient Chinese referenced this natural life force, or energy, within everything. When chi flows gently through your space, it nourishes you and revitalizes you. When we feel stressed or stuck, it is because there is an imbalance in your environment, which impacts your inner world.

Feng shui is based on the same principles as quantum physics. Science proves that everything in the universe is connected and made of energy at the subatomic level. You and I are energy. Even inanimate objects, such as furniture and clothing, are made of energy. They are composed of atoms which constantly vibrate. We can't see them with the human eye, but we know this to be true.

Everything in our homes carries an energetic vibration. Since everything is energy, everything that surrounds you, affects you. Everything in your environment will either inspire you or discourage you. Adjusting your environment using the principles of feng shui can help you to be more productive in your space and give you a greater sense of inner peace and security.

Three Types of Chi

Cosmic Chi is the force of nature. This is the universal energy that affects us all. This energy is similar to the way the earth is pulled by the sun and the way the tides are affected by the moon. This explains why our moods and energy levels are impacted by the new moon, the full moon, or the change in season.

Human Chi is your personal energy. Each person has his or her own unique chi that flows in its own path. It affects your personality, how you interact with others, and much more. Feng shui can help you nourish and strengthen your personal chi.

Earth Chi refers to how the earth affects you. Mountains, lakes, and plains will all impact your personal chi differently. We tend to feel more stable and grounded when we have a mountain behind us; whereas large bodies of water could intensify emotions.

Yin and Yang

Life is all about finding balance. You can achieve harmony in your relationships, and within yourself, by representing yin and yang elements in your space. Yin is the feminine energy represented by dark colors, and soft textures and lighting. Yang is the masculine energy represented by bright colors and patterns, sharp edges, and bright lighting.

Some rooms of your home will benefit more from Yin energy, such as your bedroom where you want to rest. The kitchen is a livelier space where you can have more Yang. Regardless, it's always good to have a little balance.

YIN	YANG
Negative	Positive
Feminine	Masculine
Passive	Active
Intuitive	Logical
Dark	Light
Cold	Hot
Night	Day
Moon	Sun

Figure 1.1

When you compare the two energies of yin and yang, one is not "better" or "worse" than the other. They both rely on each other in order to coexist. Yin, feminine energy, is on the left and represented with black. Yang, masculine energy, is on the right and represented with white. Both are equally important. Without the darkness there cannot be light. We all possess both energies, regardless of our gender. An environment will also possess these dual energies. By adjusting your space, you can influence how you feel.

Transcendental and Mundane Cures

Another duality in feng shui which helps you achieve balance are mundane and transcendental cures. You will be able to apply these in your home, office, or classroom so that they look *and* feel better. Transcendental cures address the invisible forces around us. Transcendental adjustments include symbolic gestures. They may not seem to make sense to the logical mind, but transcendental adjustments are necessary and work to improve the energy of those who implement them.

Mundane cures are the physical adjustments of feng shui. When one makes physical adjustments to the environment, such as moving a piece of furniture, de-cluttering, or adding a piece of decor, this is addressing the mundane side of feng shui. Transcendental and mundane cures work hand-in-hand to create more harmonious living and working spaces, and both will be addressed throughout this book.

Introducing the Bagua Map

Using a tool called the bagua map (See Figure 1.2), you will be able to see which area of your home, office, or classroom connects to specific areas of your life. The bagua (also called ba-gua or pakua) is one of the main tools used in feng shui to analyze the energy of any given space. The bagua comes from the sacred text, the book of *I-Ching*, which is used to predict the future and provide life advice and wisdom.

"Ba" = 8 and "Gua"= area or trigram

The map divides your space into nine different areas. The center area, or gua, is the "ninth" area with signifies the center of the home. The center of the home represents health and well-being. The center of the home is connected to all eight guas, so it is very important! When the center of the home is clear, it radiates positive energy to all other areas of your home, and your life. The surrounding areas signify the 8 areas of your life:

- Career
- Relationships
- Family
- Wealth/Abundance
- Children/Creativity
- Helpful People/Travel
- Wisdom/Self Knowledge
- Fame/Reputation

Western feng shui practitioners use the front door, or the main entrance of a space, when laying the bagua map on the floor plan of a building or room. The front door is considered "the mouth of chi." Every time you open your front door, fresh energy flows into the home and nourishes the entire house and, in effect, all areas of your life.

Ideally, a feng shui home will have good flowing energy in all nine areas, but it takes time. It is recommended to focus on one gua, or area of your home, at a time.

Wealth Colors: Purple, Green, Gold	Fame and Reputation Colors: Red	Relationship Colors: Pink, Skin tones
Family Colors: Green, Brown	Health Center Colors: Yellow, Earth tones	Children and Creativity Colors: White, Bright Pastel
Wisdom and Self Knowledge Colors: Blue-green	Career Colors: Dark Blue, Black	Helpful People and Travel Colors: Gray, Mauve

Wall that contains the main entrance

Figure 1.2 Image Credit: Apple Vert

The Five Elements

The five elements are all related to nature, and they should also be represented in your home, office, or classroom. The five elements are:

- Wood
- Fire
- Earth
- Metal
- Water

Each area of your home connects to different elements, which are represented by different colors and shapes. If you have a room that does not feel quite right, try balancing the elements to make it more comfortable. Each element invokes a different mood, creating a customized space that's beneficial for your personality and goals.

How to Represent the Five Elements

Element	Shape	Color
Wood	Vertical rectangle, pillar	Green, brown
Fire	Triangle	Red, bright orange, yellow
Earth	Square, horizontal rectangle	Sand, beige, yellow
Metal	Circle	Gray, white, bronze
Water	Odd shaped, waves	Deep blue, black

Figure 1.3

The way in which the elements are represented by shape and color reflect how the elements are portrayed in nature (See Figure 1.3). When you think of a campfire, you can visualize the flames burning upward, creating a triangular shape. The center of the fire will glow a deep red or sometimes a shade of purple, whereas the top of the fire will radiate yellow. For this reason, all elements can be represented by an ombré of colors.

All energy vibrates at different frequencies. Let's compare fire and water. When you imagine fire, you can feel the heat and the vibrant energy emitting from the flames. Now think of water. It's cool and soothing. Just like the actual elements of fire and water, the colors of fire (red) and water (blue) also give off different energy and vibrational frequencies. With this in mind, feng shui works because each area of your home is best fit for a specific element. When we honor the element of the area, or gua, we naturally feel more at peace and we activate the energy in that part of our life.

Let's say you are looking to attract more abundance into your life. The wealth area is represented by the wood element. You would want to decorate that area of your home using the shapes and colors that represent the wood element. This will nourish that zone of your home by embracing the natural vibrational frequency of that area. Using the wood or water element (which supports wood) will help you attract more abundance with ease, all while feeling more serine in the space!

Are you ready to take a chance with feng shui?

> *"A ship is always safe at shore, but that*
> *is not what it is built for."*
> *-Albert Einstein*

The knowledge of feng shui is a very powerful tool that you can use as situations arise in your life. It gives you the ability to stretch your imagination and design the life you deserve. Using the bagua map, you can address any area of life and feel the results almost instantly!

Now that you know the basic principles of feng shui, you are ready to learn how to apply them into your home or classroom. You may want to try Activity 1 "The Nine Areas of Life: Using the Bagua Map" in the Appendix. It provides you with the opportunity to lay the bagua map on your whole house or one room, and it is a great starting point!

Chapter 2
Cleaning with a Twist

"We never truly own anything in life. We are simply the caretakers of things for a while and then we must let them move on, allowing space for newness to emerge."
-Davina Mackail

Have you have noticed how much better you feel after organizing your closet or cleaning the kitchen? Cleaning and decluttering are the first steps to take before making any other feng shui enhancements. There is a saying in feng shui, "Tidy room, tidy mind. Cluttered room, cluttered mind." When you clean your space, you clear your mind.

A stack of mail or unpaid bills will subconsciously make you feel overwhelmed. When you minimize the clutter, you reduce worries such as *"I've been meaning to go through that pile of mail..."* You are able to think much clearer and with less distraction.

Although the feng shui process can be done in any order, regular cleaning and decluttering are essential, ongoing aspects of feng shui. It is the first step for any room because it is so effective. You can arrange your furniture and decorate your house in alignment with the elements, but if your space is filled with clutter or objects that represent unwanted memories, you will find it very difficult to move forward in your life and get the inner peace that you long for.

The Flow of Chi

In order to understand why decluttering and cleaning your space is so vital, you need to have a basic understanding of how chi works. Energy flows *forward*. That is why it is so important to place furniture strategically so that it circulates evenly throughout the room, giving the space life and vibrancy.

Closets, cabinets, and drawers have very stagnant energy because once the energy flows into those spaces, it gets stuck and has nowhere to go. The only cure to get the energy flowing again is to move the objects around by getting rid of items you no longer need and by opening windows to get the air circulating.

Clutter, dirt, dust and grime slow down the flow of chi, or positive energy. This is another reason cleaning regularly is so necessary for you to feel your best. Chi is the life source. When it is flowing naturally and effortlessly, it creates balance in your environment. As a result, when your environment is in harmony, you feel more internal peace.

By removing clutter and organizing your space, you can remove stumbling blocks in your life that have been holding you back. Each area of your home represents an aspect of your life. If you have a "junk room" this may not only be a space that needs to be cleaned out, but it could also be an aspect of your life that you feel needs improvement.

Cleaning with Intention

Of course you already know how to clean, but would you consider a new way of doing it? Each room in your house, including the closets, garage, and that dark corner of the basement that you've avoided forever, are all part of the bagua map. The bagua map is laid out on your floor plan and coordinates with different areas of your life. Based on this map, you can see which areas of your life you may have neglected, based on the rooms that correlate.

Just as you can see which areas you need to address, you can also use the bagua map to target the areas of your life that you want to see improve; and the first step to improvement involves cleaning with intention.

To clean with intention, you must think about why you are tending to that specific gua. What are you ready to let go of? What do you wish to attract? It is a very powerful combination when you make physical changes to your environment in conjunction with setting your intention.

When you clean with the awareness of which area of your life you are cleaning, you will feel profound results. As you clean each room in your house, be aware of which gua you are in. As you dust, vacuum, and clear out the cobwebs, think about what old beliefs you are clearing away.

Let's say you are in your living room, which happens to be in the Helpful People and Travel gua. As you clean this space, think of the helpful people that you are uncovering as you clear away the dust. Since this gua is activated by spiritual guides, you could imagine any higher powers such as angels, Buddha, Jesus, or other ascended masters whom you believe in. Feng shui is not a religion, therefore, any spiritual guides you call upon will work.

As you clean the Helpful People/Travel gua, you may also think of places you wish to go-- dream big! Even if your logical mind tells you it is not possible, you must affirm what you want. The universe responds to your intentions in extremely creative ways.

As you spend time in this Helpful People/Travel gua and clear away the old energy, you will start to feel lighter. Some of the old limiting beliefs that your ego may have been whispering in your ear such as, "it's too expensive to go on vacation... we can't afford to go there.... we don't have enough help with the kids..." will start to fade away and your new mindset will start to set in.

As you set your new intention while you clean, you open your heart and subconscious to your Higher Self, which always says "yes!" to your heart's desires. As long as your dreams and wishes are for the greater good, you will start to see opportunities open. This is cleaning with intention.

Minimize

Now that you know how to "clean with intention," you are ready for the knitty-gritty, not-always-fun-but-always-rewarding step of decluttering. Every item that surrounds you carries energy that can either inspire or discourage you.

Objects carry energetic imprints that can elevate or lower your energy. If you had a bad experience in an outfit, you are reminded of those negative feelings every time you see it or wear it. (Chances are you have subconsciously avoided that outfit for some time now). Letting go of objects that do not bring you joy can be a very empowering and uplifting experience!

Although some people tremble at the idea of decluttering because they have "so much stuff," you could start small. Select a closet that is located in an area of the bagua map that you wish to see immediate results.

I had a client who wanted to work on her self-confidence and her relationship with her husband. In order to have a well-nourished relationship, you must first know yourself, what you want, and how to ask for it. I recommended she start decluttering the closet, which was located in the Wisdom and Knowledge gua. The more time she spent in that space with the intention of "clearing her mind and connecting with herself," the more clarity she gained. When she knew what to ask for and what she wanted in her relationship, she felt like her needs were being met and her relationship was more fulfilling.

Teaching from the Heart with Feng Shui

> ### **Three Steps to Declutter**
>
> 1. Take everything out of the closet. It is going to have to get worse before it gets better!
>
> 2. Hold each object before placing it back in the closet. Feel the energy. If it is an article of clothing, how do you feel when you wear it? Do you have positive memories in that piece or did something not-so-great happen when you wore it? If the object evokes positive feelings, keep it. If not, donate it.
>
> 3. If you are on the fence about something, you could create a "maybe" pile. Place those "maybe" objects in a bag. If you don't go to the bag in the next three months to retrieve the object, then you really don't need it, and you can give it away.
>
> Cleaning and minimizing need to be done regularly in order to keep the chi flowing at its highest potential. It will also keep you feeling your best. When you clear away the dust and clutter, you open up the pathway for new inspirations and ideas.

Give Cleaning with Intention a Try!

Next time you are feeling overwhelmed or swamped with things to do, try cleaning your house. Once that is in order, the next best step will come to you much more easily! Some of my greatest ideas have come to me while I clean with intention.

You will be surprised at the profound results you can experience with such a simple concept. You may want to try Activity 2 in the Appendix "Let's Get Energized: Understanding the Flow of Chi." It will help you to plan how to arrange furniture and declutter your space so that you can create the optimal flow of nourishing chi.

Chapter 3
Applying Elemental Cures with Décor

"Your home is an affirmation for the life you desire."
-Inessa Freylekhman, Master Instructor

This is where feng shui gets *really* fun! Now that you have started to organize your space and have let go of some objects that no longer serve you, you have made room for new objects that will help you to create the life you desire. In this chapter, you will learn how to consciously select decor based on the five elements. By intentionally choosing decor based on the elements, you can enhance each area of your life based on the bagua map *and* balance your space so that it *looks* and *feels* more comfortable.

How to Represent the Five Elements

There are three ways to represent elements. When making adjustments in feng shui, here is the order in which they are most effective:

1. **The Shape of the Element**: When you use the shape of the element, the shape takes precedence over the color of the object.

   - **Earth:** square or horizontal rectangle
   - **Wood:** vertical rectangle or pillar
   - **Fire:** triangle
   - **Water:** curvy odd-shaped or wavy
   - **Metal:** circle

2. **The Color of the Element**: Let's say you have a black circular rug. The color black represents water. However, remember that the shape takes precedence, so the circular shape will also represent metal.

- **Earth:** sand colors, beige, yellow
- **Wood:** green or brown
- **Fire:** red, bright orange, purple
- **Water:** blue or black
- **Metal:** gray, white, bronze

3. **The Actual Element:** When you use the element, you are representing it.

- **Earth**: plants or flowers, granite countertops, rocks
- **Wood:** bamboo, logs, wooden frames
- **Fire:** candles, fireplace
- **Water**: fountain or fish tank
- **Metal:** metal decor or coins

Your home is an affirmation for the life you desire! As you move items around and place decorations with intention, you are proclaiming exactly what it is that you wish to attract into your life. Let's say that you place a candle to represent the fire element in the Fame and Reputation gua, and you light it each night with the intention that your boss will start to see you for the dedicated employee that you are. Every time you look at the glowing candle, you will be reminded of the valuable employee you are. Over time, you will have more confidence, and the universe will bring you exactly what you need in Divine timing in order to take the next step in your career.

Decor Suggestions to Represent Each Element

1. **Earth:** square or rectangular (horizontal) picture frames, yellow throw blanket or accent pillows, sand colored towels, sand or rocks in a square dish, a salt lamp, fresh flowers or silk flowers that look real

2. **Water:** picture of the ocean, fish tank, water fountain, thunderstorm or ocean sounds, mirrors, purple drapes

3. **Fire:** candles, fireplace, picture with reds or bright orange, Christmas tree, triangular patterns, weapons, fur, leather, feathers

4. **Wood:** rectangular frames (vertical), wooden sculptures or dishes, wood furniture, bamboo plant, money tree, bonsai tree

5. **Metal:** metal dishes, circular frames or clocks, metallic artwork, gray or white throw pillows or curtains

Figure 3.1

Use What You Have

When I conduct a feng shui consultation, I always try to see what the client already has in his or her home before I recommend making any purchases. Many times, you already have decorations such as vases, mirrors, throw pillows, and picture frames, which can be used to represent the elements. Sometimes you simply need to move a piece of artwork to another wall, or place a candle in a different room in order to activate the gua properly.

Constructive and Destructive Cycles

Are you ready to stretch your creativity and take your interior decorating to the next level? Each gua is best represented by one of the five elements, but you are not limited to those options. The elements interact with one another. Some elements support one another, such as wood supports fire. This is called a "constructive/supportive cycle." Other elements destroy each other, such as when metal cuts wood. This is known as the "destructive cycle."

Why is it beneficial to know about the constructive and destructive cycles? If you have too much of an element in one room, it can feel overwhelming or drab. You can fix this by using other colors and shapes to make the space feel more balanced. Using a combination of elements makes your space more interesting and tranquil.

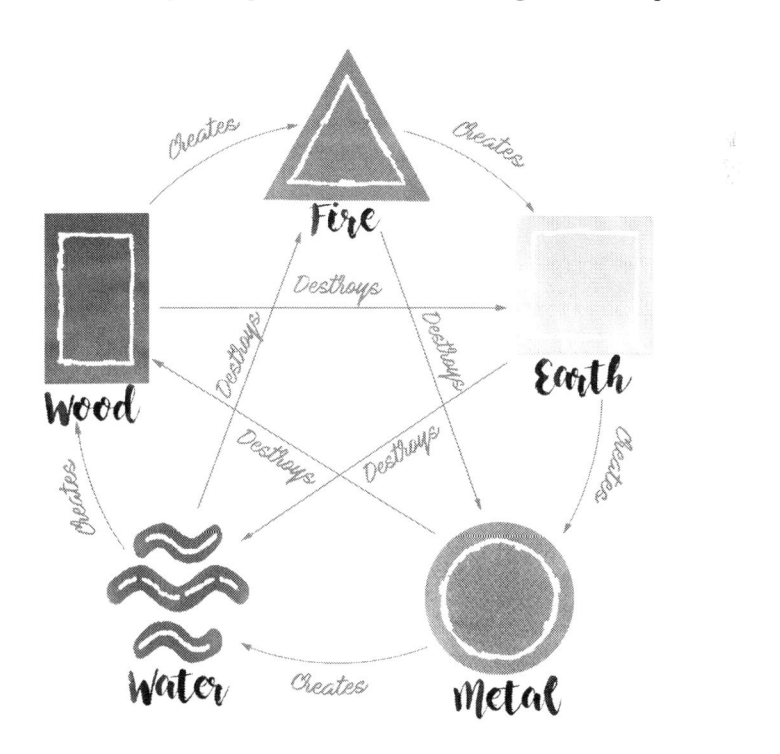

Figure 3.2 Image Credit: Apple Vert

How to Apply the Constructive/Supportive Elements

We all have our own preferences and styles when it comes to decorating. Perhaps your living room is in the Helpful People and Travel gua, but you are not a huge fan of the colors which represent metal (grays, whites, and silver). Knowing the supportive element will give you more color and shape options. In this case, you could use Earth tones in the helpful people and travel gua because Earth supports Metal.

Bagua Map with the Constructive (Supportive) Elements

Wealth	Fame/Reputation	Relationship
Element: wood *Supportive Element: water* *Supportive Shape: wavy/odd* *Supportive Colors: blue, black or mirrors to represent water*	Element: fire *Supportive Element: wood* *Supportive Shape: vertical rectangle* *Supportive Colors: green, gold, purple*	Element: Earth *Supportive Element: fire* *Supportive Shape: triangle* *Supportive Colors: red, bright orange*
Family	**Health**	**Children/Creativity**
Element: wood *Supportive Element: water* *Supportive Shape: wavy/odd* *Supportive Colors: blue, black or mirrors to represent water*	Element: Earth *Supportive Element: fire* *Supportive Shape: Triangle* *Supportive Colors: red, bright orange*	Element: metal *Supportive Element: Earth* *Supportive Shape: square or horizontal rectangle* *Supportive Colors: yellow, Earth tones*
Knowledge	**Career**	**Helpful People/ Travel**
Element: Earth *Supportive Element: fire* *Supportive Shape: triangle* *Supportive Colors: red, bright orange*	Element: water *Supportive Element: metal* *Supportive Shape: Circle* *Supportive Colors: white, bright and pastel colors, gray*	Element: metal *Supportive Element: Earth* *Supportive Shape: square or horizontal rectangle* *Supportive Colors: yellow, earth tones*

Figure 3.3 This is a chart of the bagua map with the elements that work in each space. You will see the primary element represented as well as the secondary (supportive) element that you may use to enhance this space.

How to Apply the Destructive Elements

Do you have too much of an element in one room? Even though the wealth gua is activated by the wood element, the room will feel unbalanced and intense with only wood represented. One solution when a room has too much of a certain color or element, is to add a little of each of the five elements to create harmony. A second option is that you can also "destroy" some of the element strategically so that you create a more balanced feel.

If you have a lot of wood furniture, dark browns and greens, you could tone down the wood element by adding metal, which cuts wood. Adding a circular mirror to represent the metal element and a candle to represent the fire element would balance the space.

The Chart of the Destructive and Constructive Elements gives ideas on how to create a more balanced space. Something to keep in mind; think of these elements as salt when cooking. A little bit goes a long way! Too much of a destructive element will become overpowering and ruin the "taste."

Chart of Destructive and Constructive Elements

Element	Destroy element by...	Strengthen Element by
Too much water...	Using Earth (Earth absorbs water)	Adding metal (metal holds water)
Too much wood...	Using metal (metal chops wood)	Adding water (water nourishes trees/wood)
Too much fire...	Using water (water puts out fire)	Adding wood (wood fuels fire)
Too much Earth...	Using wood (wood breaks through the ground, such as roots growing into the Earth)	Adding fire (fire produces Earth/ashes)
Too much metal...	Using fire (fire melts metal)	Adding Earth (Earth minerals form metal)

Figure 3.4

How to Balance the Elements

Which area of your home do you feel the least comfortable? Chances are, you do not enjoy this room because there is an imbalance of the elements. Where is this room located on the bagua map? Perhaps this area also signifies an area of your life which you feel needs some improvement too. It is best to focus on the elements one gua at a time. So, let's start in the first room that came to mind.

When you are thinking about how to balance the elements in your space, keep in mind the balance of yin and yang. If the room has too much yin energy, it is most likely too bland, quiet or dark. If the room has too much yang energy, it probably has too many patterns and bright colors, giving you a restless feeling. Some rooms benefit from more yin, such as your bedroom. While a child's playroom or the kitchen could be more welcoming with yang energy. Regardless of the space, it is always good to have a balance. Even the master bedroom, which should feel soft and relaxing, will benefit from a pop of red to add passion.

When I am doing a consultation, I stand in the room for a few minutes to get a feel for it. I ask the client, "How much time do you spend in this room? Do you like this area?" Their response will let me know if this is an area that needs improvement.

Before moving around any decorations and applying elemental cures, you might try to do the same thing. Sit in the room for a little while to see how you feel. It takes time to pick up on the energy of the space and realize what it needs. You will need to rely on your intuition, or your gut feeling, to know what you truly need to add to your space.

Experiencing the Difference

The first time I really used the constructive and destructive elements was after our daughter was born. We had settled into our first house, and I wanted to flex my feng shui muscles and freshen up our outdated kitchen.

Our kitchen was located in the Fame and Reputation area of our home. This space is all about how others perceive you. When this area is enhanced properly, the world views you in a positive light. As you make adjustments to this gua, you should think about how you wish people would see you.

Do you want people to find you knowledgeable? Trustworthy? Dependable? The Fame gua is an especially great area to focus on if you are looking for recognition in your career or going on a job interview. If this area is not well represented, you could be feeling underappreciated or find it difficult to attract new opportunities.

So, how does one enhance the Fame and Reputation gua? The element that activates this area is fire. Adding the colors of red, the shape of the triangle, or burning candles is good in this space.

Once you understand how the elements interact with one another, you can use your imagination and combine different colors and elements to get the results you want. When we made design choices for the kitchen, we knew we had to paint the cabinets white to update the space. White represents metal element. Metal does not necessarily enhance or destroy fire, but I knew we would not want too much metal.

The countertops we chose were granite. Granite itself comes from the Earth. The Earth and metal elements support each other. In order to tame the metal element, something else had to be done.

The kitchen naturally possesses the fire element since the stove resides in it. However, we wanted to fuel the fire element even more by bringing in the wood element. Burning wood creates more fire, and this would enhance our reputation!

We were able to find a paint color that represented the wood element: cricket. My pre-feng-shui-designer self might have scoffed at this deep green, but I knew it would help fuel the fire. Once the paint went up, it really tied the whole kitchen together, and I never looked back! For some reason, when you follow the principles of feng shui, it just works-- every time!

Did the adjustments we made in the kitchen have an impact on our fame and reputation? Within four months of updating the Fame gua, my husband was recruited to work for a new company, which led to an abundance of opportunities. He was able to get into the new field he had been wishing for, and it was all because his experience and expertise looked appealing to a recruiter and his future employer.

This was the first time I had ever done a renovation based on the principles of feng shui, and it looked and felt great! Knowing the supportive elements of fire was very helpful in this situation!

Happy Feng Shui-ing!

Now that you know how to balance the elements in different ways, you can make adjustments to your surroundings and experience an energy boost and uplifting changes.

To check your understanding of the elements, try Activity 3 "Improve Your Life with the Elements: Introduction to the Five Elements" in the Appendix. It will review the five elements and how they are represented. Most importantly, it will help you start planning which colors, décor, and furniture will fit best in your space in order to elevate the chi.

Chapter 4
Setting Your Intention for Manifestation

"The mind is everything. What you think, you become."
-Buddha

Your imagination is divine guidance which reveals to you what you are capable of achieving. Your dreams were given uniquely to you because you were meant to fulfill them. In this chapter you will learn how to overcome the biggest obstacle that stands between you and your dreams, and you will learn how to replace your fears with faith.

When you make feng shui adjustments to your environment, do it with intention in order to get the results you desire. It is important to clean and decorate with a purpose so that your actions match what it is you wish to attract into your life.

The concept that your home is a metaphor for your life is new idea to many people. You could clean the windows, or "the eyes" of your home, to see things more clearly, or place fresh flowers in the center, or "the heart" of your home, to revitalize your health. As you make symbolic changes such as these to your environment, you are setting your intention to manifest a more fulfilling life. You will start to see your life transform in beautiful, unexpected ways as you make symbolic adjustments with intention.

How Intention Worked for Me

When I first started to practice feng shui I was more focused on the aesthetic aspect, how my home would look once it was painted and

I added some new decor. After my life started shifting in big ways, I realized how powerful and effective feng shui really is!

As it turns out, I had been setting my intention as I made changes to our apartment without even realizing it. The intentions I set were powerful and caused my life to get moving in positive, unexpected directions. This was especially apparent when I tried to feng shui the master bedroom.

The master bedroom is considered one of the most important areas to start when applying feng shui principles. After all, we spend one-third of our lives in our bed sleeping. The energy of your bedroom needs to flow smoothly to nurture your personal chi so that you can function at peak efficiency and grow into your fullest potential.

My husband and I were newlyweds, and it was time to graduate from the mismatched furniture to a real-deal bedroom set, so I started shopping the Memorial Day sales. I knew that according to feng shui a solid headboard would provide a "mountain" behind us, creating a sense of security each night, providing a deeper sleep. I purchased the new headboard, and with the click of a mouse, and without even realizing it, I had set the intention of being well rested!

Next, I knew I needed two night stands so that we would see things eye-to-eye. These night stands would also promote equality in our relationship. Until this point, our bed had been against the wall with no room for two night stands! Even worse, the partner who sleeps against the wall could feel trapped. We moved the bed so it was accessible on both sides and added two night stands. Without even knowing it, I had set the intention that my husband and I would both have personal freedom in the relationship and have equal power.

After some decluttering and fresh paint, our bedroom was updated. The aroma of the fresh cherry wood filled the room with new energy. Once again, feng shui had helped me to create a more welcoming, sacred space. It was as if the room gave us a big hug every time we walked into it. By creating a relaxing sanctuary, we were able to appreciate our shared space, and we started to focus more on our relationship.

Life really started to take off into new directions after making intentional design choices in the master bedroom. Within two years of the updates, my husband accepted a promotion, we bought our first house, we had our first baby, and I started graduate school. All the expansion filled my life with more love and ambition. This was one of the first experiences in which I saw how designing with intention could make a room look *and* feel better, and it could also prompt newness to emerge in all areas of your life!

How to Set Your Intention

Throughout the feng shui process, set your intention. As you plan your adjustments, think about what you want to change. Once you have finished changing the room, seal your intention with a blessing. The more intentional and purposeful you are, the better the results will be!

Affirmations

Scientists tell us that 98% of our 60,000 thoughts are repeats from the day before (Grout, 2012). We repeat so many of the same stories to ourselves on a daily basis, why not make them positive ones? Positive affirmations are when we purposely spin a negative statement or thought into a positive one. The law of attraction suggests that like attracts like:

positive thoughts = positive feelings = positive outcomes

As Dr. Wayne Dyer reminds us, "if we focus on what's ugly, we attract more ugliness into our thoughts, and then into our emotions, and ultimately into our lives." Our feelings do not create our thoughts. *Our thoughts create our feelings.* We have the power to feel good when we choose to change our thoughts. You do not have to accept where you are if you do not like it. You can shift your mind and eventually your life will follow along the new path.

Affirmation Tips

1. **Affirmations are in the NOW:** Even if you do not have exactly what you want right now, say what you want as if you already have it. For example, if you are looking to accumulate more money so that you no longer have to be stressed out about paying off your bills, you would say, "I am grateful that I always have enough to pay my bills." Or "The universe supports me financially in everything that I do."

2. **Affirm with gratitude or a positive emotion:** When you say what you want, say it with a grateful heart. Avoid using any negative words such as "no" or "do not." For example, if you are hoping to heal your relationship with your partner or another family member you could say, "I am thankful for our lifelong friendship and joyous relationship." Or, "I find great joy in talking with my partner about my feelings. We listen to each other and feel deep fulfillment in our relationship." (See Figure 4.1 for more suggestions)

You might not believe these statements yet, but the idea is that your thoughts will eventually transform your feelings so that you can attract more of what you desire.

3. **Imagine the affirmation is true. What does it feel like?** As you say the affirmation, imagine how you would feel if this really became true. How does your body feel knowing that all is well? How do your head and heart feel now that this area of your life is healed? Say it. Mean it. Feel it.

Dr. Laura Berman has elaborate research on the study of quantum physics and how this particular step, "feeling as if," is so vital to the process of attracting what you want into your life. Your body's cells respond at the molecular level when you visualize what you want and act as if you already have it. The universe matches your vibrational frequencies and delivers exactly what it is that you are giving out.

Affirmations Aligned to the Bagua Map

Wealth	Fame/Reputation	Relationship
I am grateful for the infinite flow of abundance. The universe always takes care of me. There are unlimited resources available to me. And so it is!	I am knowledgeable and well-respected. I am hardworking and responsible. I am grateful for the abundant opportunities that are presented to me.	I am appreciated and respected by my partner. I joyfully attract the perfect partner for me. I am open to understanding my partner.
Family	**Health**	**Children/Creativity**
My family loves and supports me in everything I do. I am grateful for the connections I have within my family tree.	I have vibrant energy. My immune system is strong. Our family easily gets over colds.	My mind is open to receiving Divine guidance and creativity. My child feels nurtured and creative in this space. I easily communicate with others.
Knowledge	**Career**	**Helpful People/ Travel**
I love and appreciate myself. I am special and unique, and I have everything I need to fulfill my Divine life purpose.	I love what I do and get paid good money to do it. My career is fulfilling. I find great joy in fulfilling my Divine life purpose. I am open to receiving Divine guidance and expanding my career opportunities.	I am surrounded by helpful family and friends. Life always supports me by sending me the right people at exactly the right time. I attract helpful people into my life who can guide me in the right direction towards fulfilling my dreams. I easily and effortlessly can travel where my heart desires.

Figure 4.1 This bagua map provides sample affirmations to seal your intention and get what you want in each area of your life according to the bagua map.

Sealing with Intent

After making any external movement to your environment, you may bless the shift with a prayer from any religion that you identify with. Remember, feng shui is not a religion. It honors all beliefs, even non-believers.

There are official mudras to seal your intentions that have been passed down from the ancestors to feng shui practitioners. These mudras are only to be shared by a feng shui teacher to student or from consultant to client and cannot be written in this book. These are powerful tools that are available to you if you decide that you want to take your feng shui journey a step further. However, I was unaware of these mudras when I first started to apply feng shui, and I experienced many joyous shifts regardless. Your personal prayers and affirmations are still very powerful, and you will experience accelerated results by setting your intention in your own unique way.

Embracing Affirmations Everyday

In this chapter you learned how to seal the deal! You learned the importance of sharing your intentions so that you can attract into your life that which you desire and deserve. You can use affirmations as a way to clarify your intentions for any feng shui adjustment. You can start using positive affirmations on a daily basis to shift from the negative stories we tell ourselves to more uplifting ones.

Part II
Feng Shui in the Classroom

Chapter 5
The Research Supporting Feng Shui in Schools

"In any given moment we have two options; to step forward into growth or to step back into safety."
-Abraham Maslow

Feng shui is a technique that will help you integrate your personal and professional life so that you feel inner peace throughout your day, no matter where you are. Some people spend more time in their classroom or office than they do in their own home; so it is vital that you feel like your workspace is your home-away-from-home.

If you are a stay-at-home parent or have a home-based office, it is even more important to apply feng shui to your house so that you feel serenity throughout your day and have a separation between work, play and relaxation.

My Feng Shui Classroom Saved Me

My family and I recently went through some unforeseen circumstances. Feng shui can help you cope with problems as they arise, but unfortunately it cannot make you immune to them! Having a classroom which felt tranquil and serene really helped me get through this challenging time in our lives...

Just as we had sold our first house in less than three days, and put an offer on our "dream home," my husband lost his job. We could no longer qualify for the new house, and I was four months pregnant with our second child. We were faced with a very difficult decision.

Should we continue with the sale of our house and find temporary housing while we figured things out, or should we stay in a house that we had outgrown and wait for the dust to settle?

Many factors were taken into consideration as we pondered our decision. Abraham Maslow once said, "In any given moment we have two options; to step forward into growth or to step back into safety." We decided to take a leap of faith in the direction of our dreams. We sold our home and moved into an apartment until the next steps became clear.

Although this situation brought a lot of fear and uncertainty, feng shui helped me through it. When I entered my classroom, I felt relieved knowing that the students would elevate the energy because of the culture we had established over the course of the school year. This is how my feng shui classroom revived me during a very challenging time.

We have all had life throw us unexpected surprises. If you don't have a strategy, your personal life can consume you so much that you are unable to show up as your best self for your students, colleagues, or family. This is where feng shui can help you. As you learn how to apply feng shui in any given environment, you can make small actions that will calm your energy and give you greater clarity when you need it most. When you feel better, you are able to give more of yourself to others.

How Could Feng Shui Help Your Classroom?

The week before school begins, the teachers set up their classrooms with the intention of starting the year fresh. Whether they know it or not, they are practicing feng shui.

When the students clean out their desks on Fridays or help organize the classroom library, they too are practicing feng shui. Feng shui is not a fancy tool that is only for elite master practitioners. It is easily accessible to everyone, and it is simple to apply once you know the basics.

Feng shui is a gateway to giving teachers, administrators, and students the opportunity to become more aware of their internal and external world. It empowers those who practice it to function at their highest potential. It increases productivity, clarity, and feelings of inner peace.

Anxiety can be reduced by making feng shui adjustments on a daily basis. Some adjustments are as simple as dusting a desk or discarding a pile of old papers which are no longer needed. Other adjustments take a little more thought and consideration, such as moving a desk to another side of the room to allow the chi to flow more smoothly and to give the occupant a better view.

The way the school is designed and organized affects student achievement. Schools around the world are starting to realize the impact that the classroom environment has on student success. Ashley Rose (2016) reported in the article *Classroom Feng Shui:*

> "According to a study done by the University of Salford Manchester in the United Kingdom and architects of Nightingale Associates, the classroom environment can affect a child's academic progress over a year by as much as 25 percent… The study was done in seven primary schools in Blackpool, England. There were 34 classrooms with different learning environments and age groups which took part. Data was taken from 751 students, such as their age, gender, and performance levels in math, reading, and writing at the beginning of the year and end of the school year. They studied the classroom environment, taking into account

different design parameters such as classroom orientation, natural light and noise, temperature, and air quality. They also looked at flexibility of space, storage facilities, organization and the use of color. According to the study, 'Current findings suggest that placing an average pupil in the least effective, rather than the most effective classroom environment could affect their learning process by as much as the average improvement across one year. Notably, 73 percent of the variation in pupil performance driven at the class level can be explained by the building environment factor measured in this study.'"(p. 3)

According to the University of Salford Manchester study, almost three quarters of the student performance variations were impacted by the classroom environment. The colors, furniture arrangement, temperature and lighting all impacted their academic achievement. Studies like this have fueled many educational leaders to reconsider how they redesign buildings, and teachers are starting to become more aware of how they arrange and organize their classrooms.

Although some teachers or administrators may be hesitant about introducing the "new" concept of feng shui, it must be noted that feng shui does not violate anyone's religious beliefs. Feng shui is *not* a religious practice. "The First Amendment Center, which works to preserve and protect First Amendment freedoms through information and education, has approved the organizational tips embodied by feng shui. Feng shui does not infringe upon anyone's freedom of religion. If the environment is balanced students will learn easier." (Heiss, 2004)

With the basic knowledge of feng shui, educational professionals can manipulate the classroom environment without investing thousands or millions of dollars. There are simple changes that educators can implement immediately. Adjusting the shades for more natural light, rearranging furniture, and updating bulletin boards with intentional color schemes are just a few feng shui "quick fixes" that can make a huge improvement.

The Danielson Connection

Researchers within the field of education are starting to realize the impact the classroom environment has on student learning. Many school districts have adopted Charlotte Danielson's framework as a way to promote an ongoing dialogue between administrators and teachers and to influence teachers to be more reflective. Within the framework there are four domains in which teachers demonstrate proficiency: Planning and Preparation, Classroom Environment, Professional Responsibilities, and Instruction. Each domain is broken down into several key components in which teachers are rated by the following scale: unsatisfactory, basic, proficient, and distinguished (See Figure 5.1)

Although feng shui is not mentioned in the Danielson Framework, there are principles of feng shui that can be applied to the classroom setting in order to demonstrate proficiency and, moreover, improve the classroom environment and quality of instruction.

Under Domain 2, the Classroom Environment, there is Component 2E: Organizing Physical Space. Danielson suggests, "Use of physical space is important in a total learning environment; the physical surrounding can have a material effect on interactions or the structure of activities," (Danielson, p.73, 2007). The way a teacher organizes, decorates, and arranges his classroom, has an impact on how the students feel and how they interact with one another.

Domain 2: The Classroom Environment

Component 2E: Organizing Physical Space	Level of Performance
Element (Description): Arrangement of furniture and use of physical resources	**Unsatisfactory:** The furniture arrangement hinders the learning activities, or the teacher makes poor use of physical resources. **Basic:** Teacher uses physical resources adequately. The furniture may be adjusted for a lesson, but with limited effectiveness. **Proficient:** Teacher uses physical resources skillfully, and the furniture arrangement is a resource for learning activities. **Distinguished:** Both teacher and students use physical resources easily and skillfully, and students adjust the furniture to advance their learning.

Figure 5.1 This table describes the levels of performance for Component 2E of the Danielson Framework (Danielson, p.76, 2007).

Not only are teachers encouraged to be aware of how they organize the classroom, but, according to the Danielson Framework, students are encouraged to take ownership of the classroom. When it comes to Domain 2, The Classroom Environment, the "Distinguished" teacher provides opportunities for the students to take responsibility of the safety, accessibility, and arrangement of furniture and physical resources. Danielson states:

> "When a classroom is a true community of learners, students themselves become involved in the physical environment and take initiative in making it effective. They may, for example, plan a display of work, move furniture to facilitate a group project, or shift supplies to improve the traffic flow. They may lower the shades to block the sun from classmates' eyes or shut the door to keep out the noise." (p.75)

Danielson suggests the "Distinguished" teacher is one who creates an environment in which the students feel comfortable enough to make adjustments to the space. In order for students to take ownership of the classroom and make these types of ongoing changes, the instructor needs to have ongoing dialogue with the students about how to take pride and ownership in the classroom. The teacher needs to give the students time to organize their personal belongings, as well as help with community materials in the classroom.

Renovating Schools with Feng Shui

Schools such as Alvarado Junior High School are also recognizing the need to create classroom environments that are more conducive to learning. Learning by Design recognized the newly renovated school with a 2016 Outstanding Project award in the Middle School/Intermediate School category. Huckabee & Associates is the architectural firm that designed the building which reinforced the school's vision to support 21st century learners by including spaces for collaboration and creative thinking activities.

According to Learning by Design, "the design of AJHS was influenced by staff who wanted to push the envelope and create new standard for instructional delivery," (Rose, 2016, p.2). Educators are realizing how the classroom environment impacts student learning; it can either support or hinder the new wave of technology and instruction.

Feng Shui in Schools: The New Normal

Could feng shui fit into the mainstream future of our schools? The first step when applying feng shui is to emphasize the importance of decluttering and cleaning the classroom on a regular basis. If this was a priority in schools, the classroom environments would naturally improve.

There are already schools that are adopting the feng shui philosophy by hiring professionals such as Jane Anderson (2010), author of *The Decluttered School*. She was a feng shui consultant for organizations such as IKEA and the National Health Service. As a feng shui practitioner she has also worked with many school districts throughout the UK to help them declutter. According to Anderson, decluttering is the "in-thing" for various reasons.

Decluttering is...

- immediate.
- effective; what you end up with afterwards is always better than what you had before.
- inexpensive.
- very satisfying.
- inclusive and a great team builder. (p.8)

Clutter affects the ability of teachers and students to concentrate and feel peaceful. A pile of ungraded papers in plain sight could cause anxiety for the instructor and keep her from the present moment. A mound of unused books from three decades ago carries stagnant energy, when there could be something more uplifting and motivating in its place.

Empowering Children with Feng Shui

Keeping a "feng shui classroom" has brought my students and I together. We all do our parts to keep the classroom functioning and uplifting. I spray lavender smudge spray when I start to feel tension or the room gets an interesting scent. I open the windows to let fresh air rejuvenate the space, even if it is only for a few minutes. The students remind me to pull the shades back up if I had to draw them for a special presentation since the room feels better when the natural sunlight flows in.

My class and I have established routines that support a culture of collaboration and respect for our classroom. The students rotate jobs weekly. They help dust the surfaces of desks, countertops and book shelves, and they look forward to cleaning out their desks and lockers each Friday. They enjoy these procedures so much that they will remind me when it is time to do them!

My students and I take pride in our classroom environment, and we get compliments on it all the time. If I love coming to work so much, and my students have such a positive experience with feng shui, surely other teachers could benefit from trying it in their classrooms too!

Chapter 6
Creating Flow in Your Classroom

"Learning how to transform energy is so important. It should be taught along with reading, writing, and arithmetic."
-Pam Grout, E-Squared

Do you remember your favorite teacher? Did you love her classroom too? My fourth grade teacher made the greatest impact on me. At the beginning of the year Mrs. Dykstra announced, "This classroom is like your second home. Some of you will spend more time here throughout the day than at your own house. I want us all to respect the classroom as if it is your home." Looking back, I realize that she set the tone for the whole year with those words, and I never forgot how welcomed she made me feel.

Some students experience chaos and disorder when they return to their homes each night. As teachers, we have the opportunity to create an environment and classroom culture where all students feel a sense of security and inner-peace when they are at school.

Everything is Energy

Feng shui supports the belief that everything carries energy, including people and objects. The principles of feng shui work to create a free flow of energy so that it is not too stagnant or too rambunctious.

Teachers know from personal experience that when there are piles of ungraded papers it feels more stressed. A stack of unfinished work carries the energy that you associate with it. Every time you look at the work, your thoughts create the feeling of anxiety. If you clear the clutter and place it in a designated location, you will feel better almost instantly.

Children and teenagers are also sensitive to their environments. When there are too many distractions around, they struggle to focus. It is our job as adults to provide the most supportive, harmonious environment so that everyone can function at peak efficiency.

As you will discover, feng shui provides ways to manipulate the energy in your surroundings. Some of the suggestions will be easy to apply with students, and you do not even need to mention the term "feng shui" if you do not feel comfortable.

How you choose to use the techniques in your classroom is up to you. The important thing is that you are taking the steps to make your classroom feel more serine, and you are giving your students bits of knowledge to teach them how powerful they truly are!

Creating Optimal Flow

You are ready to rearrange your classroom according to the principles of feng shui! This chapter will explain how to feng shui your classroom in the following order:

- Adding yin energy
- Arranging and decluttering the teacher's desk
- Arranging the students' desks and other furniture
- How to establish decluttering and cleaning routines with students

How to Add Yin Energy to Your Classroom

The classroom already has a lot of *yang*, or active energy, by nature. Your vibrant students possess *yang* energy. The computers and fluorescent lights also produce active energy. You can find balance in your classroom by adding *yin*, or soft elements, to the environment:

- Play soft classical or new-age music in the background during work time, especially if the lights are on.
- Consider turning the lights down during independent work time.
- If your school allows, use aromatherapy with a diffuser. Lavender will calm everyone, and citrus scents encourage alertness. If you don't have a diffuser, you could place a bowl of fresh orange peels on your desk. Once they wilt, they no longer have a potent smell, so you will need to replace them.
- Pops of color and patterns are beneficial in some areas of the classroom, and they are necessary so that the space does not feel sluggish. However, t*oo much* red, pink, and pattern could be over-stimulating.

Sage Spray and Other Energy Clearing Techniques

It is an ongoing process to keep your classroom feeling light and calm. Everyone carries their own personal energy which will continually affect the overall chi in the classroom. In order to refresh your classroom, you can conduct mini space clearings in your classroom when the students are out of the room.

- Use lavender sage spray any time! It smells delightful, and it clears the energy after any stressful situation.
- When the students are not in the room, go around the classroom and clap your hands from low to high to break up the stagnant energy.
- Open a window to let in fresh air at least once a week. However, with twenty to thirty pupils in a room every day, it is probably best to let fresh energy in daily. This will circulate the chi and rejuvenate the space.

How to Use Feng Shui Crystals in the Classroom

You can protect your own personal energy and prevent yourself from feeling drained as well. The feng shui faceted quartz crystals are very powerful. They have a similar effect as Himalayan salt lamps or fresh flowers. Like the lamps and flowers, the crystals soak up negative energy and give off fresh, positive chi. They can clear any negative energy and deflect harsh energy from computers or people's negative vibes.

You could carry the crystal in your pocket for protection. You might also place a crystal on top of the SMART board projector and computer carts to deflect the harsh energy that electronics emit.

You can also hang a crystal from the ceiling above the area you wish to neutralize. Cut a nine-inch red thread and loop it through the crystal. Hang it in any area of your classroom or office that you would like to see improvements. If you are located near a busy road, you may consider hanging a crystal in the window, or placing it on the ledge of the window, for protection and to calm the energy of the room.

Clear Desk, Clear Mind

The best place to start feng shui in the classroom is at your own personal desk. If you are like most teachers, you probably do not spend that much time there. However, when you are at your desk you are probably doing some important documentation or planning that needs your full attention. Make your desk inviting and clear so that your mind feels lighter and you can focus with greater ease.

Empty each drawer one at a time. Drawers carry very stagnant energy because there is nowhere for the energy to escape. The best way to refresh the energy of the desk and release old chi is by removing objects and getting rid of what you no longer need. There are probably many teachers or students who could benefit from some old supplies that you no longer use.

Placing the Teacher's Desk in the Power Position

Arranging yourself in the power position throughout the day is very important. It gives you the most strength and energetic support. You can situate yourself in a power position at your desk or wherever you are sitting in the classroom. If you are like me, you might have multiple areas that you sit to work with students. Consider all of the seats that you frequently occupy and see if they are in the power position (See Figure 6.1).

First, you will want to able to see the door from where you are sitting. If your back is against the door, you could get startled if someone walks up behind you. You will have more peace of mind knowing exactly who is entering your space.

Is your desk towards the front or back of the classroom? Ideally you want your desk to be towards the back. This school year, I moved my desk from the relationship corner to the wealth corner. Those are the preferred guas since they are considered the most powerful, anchoring positions. Although there is a window at my back, I have a much better view of the door.

As always, you will want to make adjustments every few months to keep the chi flowing. If your desk has been in the same position for a couple years, simply turning the desk to face another direction can shift the energy. Whenever you move furniture, it freshens the chi and gives you a new perspective on life and your classroom.

How to Sit in the Power Position
1. You want to see the entrance of the room from where you sit.
2. Have your back to a solid wall if possible. If there is a window at your back, consider placing a feng shui crystal on the windowsill to give you more energetic support.
3. The further away you are from the door, the more energy you will have. If you lay the bagua map on your classroom, the wealth and relationship corners are considered "power positions" and carry the most strength.

Figure 6.1

Five Tips for Arranging Student Desks and Other Furniture

You can arrange the rest of the furniture in the classroom to enhance flow of chi. You and your students will be able to focus better when the energy circulates unobstructed throughout the classroom. Before you start moving everything around, there are some key points to remember when arranging your space:

Round is the Way: Chi flows best around curved edges. If you arrange desks in a formation that creates a lot of straight lines and sharp turns, the energy will not flow as well.

Imagine Energy as a Stream: Energy is constantly moving in a forward motion. The energy flows in each time you open your classroom door. Imagine the energy as a stream of water. As it flows in through the classroom, where would the "water" flow quickly? Would it get stuck in a certain space? Arrange the space the best you can so that the "water" does not get blocked and flows as smoothly as possible. This is another reason why opening up a window at least once a week is important. When you open the window, it allows stagnant energy to exit and refreshing chi to enter and revitalize your space.

Mountain Behind You: You want a mountain behind you. As the instructor, you need the power position so that you feel confident when working with the students. I have a couple of tables in my classroom where I meet with small groups of students for literature discussions and other activities. I have placed my chair so that my back is to the wall, and I have an unobstructed view of the whole classroom. In particular, you should be able to see the door from where you sit.

Use the Elements: As you decide where to place furniture, remember that each gua is best activated with a specific shape. One of the tables I use for small group instruction is a kidney shape. The rounded shape could represent metal, so I placed this table in the Children & Creativity gua. Another big table is a long horizontal rectangle. This shape represents the Earth element, and it is placed in the Relationship gua with an even number of chairs. The relationship corner is best activated with pairs of objects, or even numbers. This promotes partnership and successful collaboration.

No Space is Ever "Fixed" for Good: Although your classroom can stay in the same formation all year, it is best for students to switch desks every four or five weeks. Even if the desks are in the same formation, the simple movement will boost the energy. Additionally, your students will appreciate the change of perspective. They will be more alert and recharged. You could even shift your desk if you are starting to feel drained in your day-to-day activities. Many times your students will naturally ask to switch desks when they start to feel bored; a sure sign the energy is becoming stagnant!

> **Bonus Tip:** If you have a student that talks a lot and distracts others during lessons, consider placing her desk in a location where there is no "mountain", or solid wall, behind her. This will give the student less power and control of the classroom. For example, she would be best situated in Student Group A or B in Figure 6.2

Sample Classroom Arrangement

Every classroom is different, but Figure 6.2. shows an example of how I strategically arranged my classroom this school year. I used the elements, and the five suggestions above to help me make my design choices.

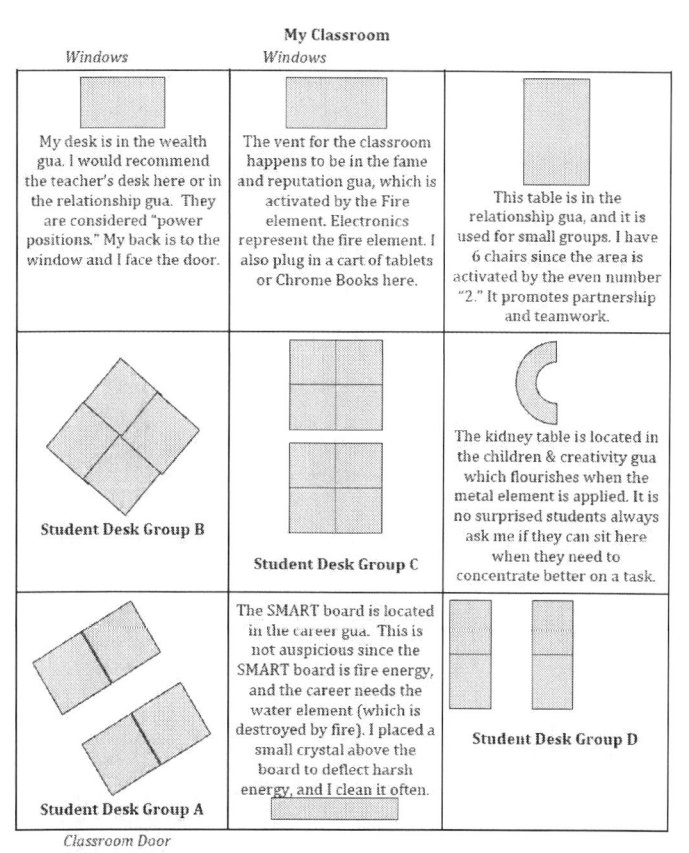

My Classroom

Windows	Windows	
My desk is in the wealth gua. I would recommend the teacher's desk here or in the relationship gua. They are considered "power positions." My back is to the window and I face the door.	The vent for the classroom happens to be in the fame and reputation gua, which is activated by the Fire element. Electronics represent the fire element. I also plug in a cart of tablets or Chrome Books here.	This table is in the relationship gua, and it is used for small groups. I have 6 chairs since the area is activated by the even number "2." It promotes partnership and teamwork.
Student Desk Group B	Student Desk Group C	The kidney table is located in the children & creativity gua which flourishes when the metal element is applied. It is no surprised students always ask me if they can sit here when they need to concentrate better on a task.
Student Desk Group A	The SMART board is located in the career gua. This is not auspicious since the SMART board is fire energy, and the career needs the water element (which is destroyed by fire). I placed a small crystal above the board to deflect harsh energy, and I clean it often.	Student Desk Group D

Classroom Door
Figure 6.2

Student Desks (in Figure 6.2):

Group A: The students are on an angle so that it creates a more "rounded" configuration. This allows the chi to flow. All students are facing the SMART board and can see the classroom door. The students are not in a group of four, but they all have a partner. When I want students to work in groups, they can move to the large worktables or turn their chairs. Also, try not to have students in line with the door. As chi enters the door, the energy rushes in. Group A is not recommended for your students who are hyperactive or have difficulty concentrating. This space has active chi because of the door, so keep this in mind when placing students here.

Group B: This group of four students are on an angle so that nobody has their back to the SMART board and everyone can see the door. Again, the angle also helps the energy flow.

Group C: The two groups in the center of the room have their backs to the East and West walls. Everyone can see the door. Although no one is facing the door or SMART board, if they look to the side they can see them. The group is not angled, but the center of the room is a "grounding" point. The center is the Health gua, and is represented by the Earth. The desks create the square, which represents the Earth element.

Group D: All students in group D have their backs to the wall. The solid wall creates a "mountain" behind them. It is very auspicious any time you can have a solid wall or chair behind you. The solid back creates support and boosts confidence and productivity.

Checklist for Student Desks

- **Is there a solid wall behind you and your students?**
- **Can your students see the classroom door?**
- **Do the desks allow optimal flow of chi, or are they creating sharp turns?**

Three Tips to Get Your Students Organized

You have worked hard to clear your classroom of unnecessary clutter and arrange the furniture for optimal energy flow. Now, the key is to stay organized and keep your classroom functioning at peak efficiency. Here are three quick tips that will help the students take ownership of the classroom and accept the responsibility of maintaining the positive vibes. If you are a teacher who is evaluated based on the Charlotte Danielson framework, this area could be used as evidence of managing your classroom environment.

Friday Desk Cleaning: It sounds so easy, but how many times do you allow your students to clean out their desks? We get so busy, that sometimes this only happens once a quarter! Try to give your students 5 minutes every week to clean out their desks. The mess in their desks causes unnecessary chaos in their minds. When the students have time to organize their personal space, they will be more efficient, remember their homework, and feel calmer. In addition, when all of the desks are organized, the overall chi of the classroom is improved.

Classroom Jobs: Many teachers assign classroom jobs. Do you have the students dust the bookshelves, counters, and common-area tables? My students love doing these types of jobs. Use whatever products your school approves, and notice how much fresher the room feels. Your classroom's chi will be heightened immediately. Do this weekly. If possible, open up the windows at the same time the students clean the surfaces. This will really boost the effectiveness as you let fresh air elevate the chi.

Teach Your Students How to Organize: Do you spend time with your students finding a "home" for every school supply? Students need direct instruction on exactly where everything goes. At the beginning of the year, I teach my students to put all of their pens, pencils and erasers in their pencil pouch, and they learn that their scissors, glue and crayons belong in their art box. We review these types of organizational procedures on a regular basis.

During our Friday Desk Cleaning, we review where everything goes. My famous line is, "There should be no loose papers in your desk. Remember, everything has a home. Put papers that need to go home in your Take Home Folder. Place papers that you still need at school in your Stay at School Folder, and anything that you don't need can be recycled." Even high school students need reminders of how to organize their space. They too need to understand the value of keeping their personal space clean.

Embracing a Positive Classroom Culture

As you read some of the classroom feng shui suggestions, there are probably many principles that you already implement. However, with the demands in curriculum and all the other aspects of education, it is easy to forget the importance of an organized classroom.

Although it is best to introduce these procedures at the beginning of the school year, it is never too late to teach your students how to be self-sufficient and embrace the responsibility of creating a cleaner, more tranquil classroom environment. Students enjoy being a part of the classroom community. As teachers, it is our job to teach them how to be a proactive participant.

Before moving on to the next chapter, you might want to check out the Appendix and try Activity 5 "Let's Find More Balance: Yin & Yang." It gives you the chance to evaluate your understanding of how yin and yang can be represented and promoted.

Chapter 7
Applying the Elements to the Classroom

*"When you change the way you look at things,
the things you look at change."*
-Dr. Wayne Dyer

When you feng shui your classroom or office, the effect is two-fold. You will improve all nine areas of your personal life as well as your professional life. Not to mention, your students will also benefit from the free-flowing, revitalizing energy. In the last chapter we focused on the organization and functionality of the classroom. When you apply the elements to the classroom, you are really focusing on creating an inviting, eye-appealing space.

Whether or not we admit it, the way the classroom appears has a major impact on how well students focus. The aesthetics of the classroom affects how students feel when they are in the classroom, and it ultimately will determine how they feel about coming to school and learning. Students will come to school ready to work for you when they feel like their classroom is a second home. When they take ownership and pride in the classroom, magical results occur.

This school year I adjusted my bulletin board paper and borders to represent the colors of each gua. You don't have to believe in feng shui to visually see that my classroom looks vibrant and serene because of the variety of colors that I have used. Your classroom will be more harmonious if you balance the colors, avoiding too much of any one color. Once you learn how to apply elements to your classroom, you will have great flexibility in your decorating, and your students will feel the difference.

How to Activate Each Gua of Your Classroom with the Elements

Which area of your life do you really want to improve? Try updating a bulletin board in this area first. Let's say you want to improve your relationship with your spouse. You could change the bulletin board in the relationship area of your classroom or office. Assuming you have applied feng shui to the relationship area of your house, you are now maximizing your intention. You will see results sooner, and you will feel even more empowered about your current situation. Updating the relationship gua in your classroom will also have a positive impact on your students. By applying the elements in this area, you are promoting better partnerships and collaboration among your students.

Next time you are looking to update a bulletin board in your classroom, consciously select bulletin board paper and borders that will activate the gua in which it is located (See Figure 7.1). The better you align each gua with the elements, the more balanced your personal and professional life will feel. As you create the board, be aware of which gua you are working with and set your intention for the improvements you wish to make. Your desires for improvement could pertain to both your professional and personal life.

Bagua Map (BTB Feng Shui)

Wealth	Fame/Reputation	Relationship
Element: wood Shape: vertical rectangle Colors: green, gold, purple *Activating the wealth in your classroom will bring you an abundance of time, money or whatever else you need. Set your intention and open your arms to receive!	Element: fire Shape: triangle Colors: red, bright orange *Activating the fame and reputation in your classroom will improve how your colleagues, students and parents view you.	Element: Earth Shape: square or horizontal rectangle Colors: pink, skin tones, Earth tones * Activating the relationship in your classroom will improve how your students interact with each other. It will also improve the relationship you have with your colleagues and boss.
Family Element: wood Shape: vertical rectangle Colors: green, brown *Activating the family gua will strengthen the family-like atmosphere. Your students will feel like they are part of a team.	**Health** Element: Earth Shape: square or horizontal rectangle Colors: yellow, Earth tones *Chances are that you will not have a bulletin board in the center of your classroom. You can activate health simply by standing here and stating your intention.	**Children/Creativity** Element: metal Shape: circle Colors: white, bright and pastel colors, gray *Activating creativity will increase the students' ability to concentrate and create. It will open their minds to new ideas and higher level thinking skills.
Knowledge Element: Earth Shape: square or horizontal rectangle Colors: turquoise, blues *Activating knowledge will help your students retain information, and it will help you make instructional decisions with more clarity.	**Career** Element: water Shape: wavy/odd Colors: blue or black *Activating career will help you and your students recognize your strengths. You will become more aware of your life purpose.	**Helpful People/ Travel** Element: metal Shape: circle Colors: white, gray * Activating the helpful people will bring more outside assistance for you and your students so that you can feel more supported and successful.

FRONT DOOR ENTRANCE LOCATED ON THIS WALL

Figure 7.1 This table outlines the outcomes you could experience if you apply the elemental cures in your classroom to each area on the bagua map.

Change the Decor Throughout the Year

Energy loves to move! After a few weeks, if the decor stays the same, the energy becomes stagnant. It can be very time consuming to change the background and border of bulletin boards, but there are other ways that you can reactivate a gua without completely changing the bulletin board paper. The best thing you can do to freshen up the decor in the classroom is to display student work and rotate it every few weeks.

There are many benefits to displaying student work. It demonstrates to them that their work is valued and they feel proud when they see their products showcased. When students know that their work will be on display, they work extra hard to do it correctly.

It is important to display work that is done correctly, so that it is a positive example. If there are some errors on the student's work, you could ask them to correct it before hanging it up. The student will look at her work on the wall and always remember the adjustment she made to improve it. As a result, she will more likely apply these corrections to other assignments in the future.

As you move through each unit, your bulletin boards could exemplify what the students have learned which will help them retain the lessons. Updating the students' work will keep the energy fresh and flowing in your classroom. Rejuvenating the energy helps everyone focus better in the space.

Attract What You Want... with Your Desk?

Did you know that you can place the bagua map on your desk? You can elevate the energy of all nine areas of your life simply by cleaning and organizing your desk with your intention.

Once your desk has been organized, you are ready to minimize the surface of the desk. Start by taking everything off and dusting the surface. Next, place your items strategically based on the bagua

Teaching from the Heart with Feng Shui

map and the elements that represent each gua. (See Figure 2.1) For example, I like to place a bamboo plant on the upper left corner of my desk. The upper left gua is the wealth gua, activated by the wood element. The bamboo symbolizes wood and represents upward growth. The hollowness of the bamboo signifies the openness to receive abundance. The chart below shows the bagua map and suggestions for each gua. Remember that the element is most effectively represented by the shape.

If you are conscious of the bagua map as you organize your desk and classroom, it will help you create greater harmony. The bagua map is the same as the one you place on your house, but there are some additional suggestions on how each gua specifically affects your classroom or career path.

Applying the Bagua Map to Your Desk

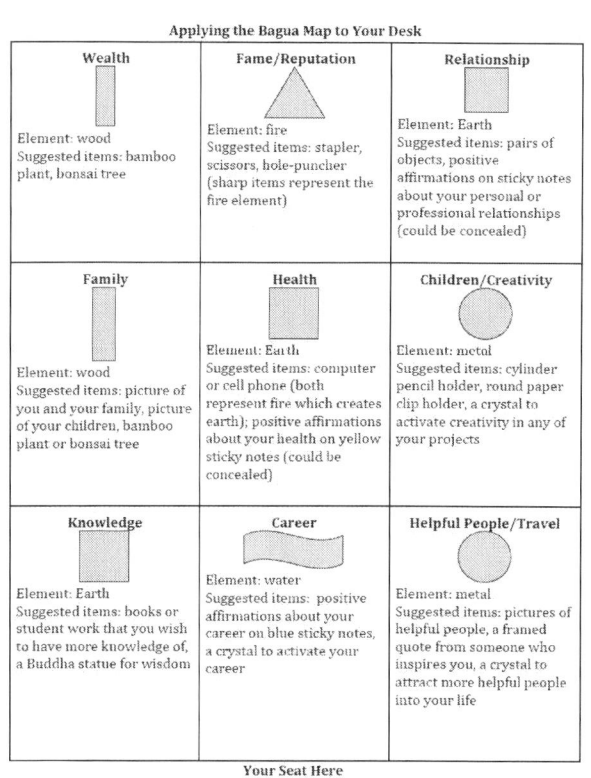

Wealth	Fame/Reputation	Relationship
Element: wood Suggested items: bamboo plant, bonsai tree	Element: fire Suggested items: stapler, scissors, hole-puncher (sharp items represent the fire element)	Element: Earth Suggested items: pairs of objects, positive affirmations on sticky notes about your personal or professional relationships (could be concealed)
Family	**Health**	**Children/Creativity**
Element: wood Suggested items: picture of you and your family, picture of your children, bamboo plant or bonsai tree	Element: Earth Suggested items: computer or cell phone (both represent fire which creates earth); positive affirmations about your health on yellow sticky notes (could be concealed)	Element: metal Suggested items: cylinder pencil holder, round paper clip holder, a crystal to activate creativity in any of your projects
Knowledge	**Career**	**Helpful People/Travel**
Element: Earth Suggested items: books or student work that you wish to have more knowledge of, a Buddha statue for wisdom	Element: water Suggested items: positive affirmations about your career on blue sticky notes, a crystal to activate your career	Element: metal Suggested items: pictures of helpful people, a framed quote from someone who inspires you, a crystal to attract more helpful people into your life

Your Seat Here

Figure 7.2 This figure provides examples of how to represent the five elements on your desk according to the bagua map.

Why Teach the Elements to Kids?

Teaching your students or children about the ways the elements interact can empower them to take ownership of their space and create the life they desire. Just as adults want to reach their goals and feel inner peace, so do children. They need to know that if they feel uneasy, insecure, or unhappy, they have the power to do something about it!

If a classroom or bedroom has an imbalance of the elements, it can lead to stress. You and your students will think much clearer if there is more harmony among the elements. Here is a chart that shows the effects of what "too much" of each element could do.

Too much...	May cause...
Fire	Aggression, aggravation and stress
Earth	Feeling too grounded, stuck in your old ways, sluggish
Wood	Inflexibility, stuck
Water	Emotional, sensitive, overactive
Metal	Headaches, anxiety, unrest

Figure 7.3

Just as too much of an element can be undesirable, too little of an element can also have a negative impact. For example, if you don't have any Earth representation in your space, you may feel like you are unable to put all of your great ideas into practice. You might feel very emotional and passionate about something, but when it comes to implementing your ideas, you struggle to make them come to form in practical terms. Balancing the elements will help you remove stumbling blocks and get your life moving.

Before You Go

Before you move on to the next chapter, you may want to try Activity 3 in the Appendix, "Improve Your Life with the Elements: Introduction to the Five Elements." It gives you a chance to test your understanding of the elements, and you can start planning what colors and shapes would fit in certain areas of your space. Once you start applying the elements, the possibilities are endless. Enjoy creating, and watch in amazement as your surroundings starts to look *and* feel better!

Chapter 8
Positive Self-Talk and Mindfulness in the Classroom

"I don't ask you to be perfect, I just ask you to be present."
-Joe Maddon, Chicago Cubs Coach 2016

It is so important to teach your students and your children how powerful their minds are. They can create their reality by thinking about what they wish to attract into their lives. Just as we have our students set academic goals for literacy and numeracy, we can have them set personal goals in other areas of their life.

Many students are facing challenges in their personal lives that we know nothing about. You can empower children by teaching them how to deal with their issues using positive self-talk, and show them that they have the ability to achieve anything they put their minds to. They may have to work extra hard. They may need to study more or get involved in extracurricular activities, but they have the capacity to fulfill their dreams.

Louise Hay and Kristina Tracy (2008) wrote *I Think, I Am!* This book uses kid friendly language and examples of how they can use affirmations to improve their lives. Affirmations are when you take a negative thought, and turn it into a positive one. Even if you feel like saying "I can't do this," you can stay something like, "I am learning new things every day. I am capable of anything I put my mind to." The book suggests several tips for completing affirmations (See Figure 8.1).

How to Say an Affirmation
1. Always start an affirmation with positive words such as: *I can, I am, I do, I have.*
2. Say your affirmation over and over, whenever you think of it.
3. Say an affirmation especially when you are having a lot of unhappy thoughts.
4. Write down your affirmations in a notebook or journal.
5. Close your eyes and picture what you want-- this is an affirmation.

Figure 8.1

When you teach children how to change negative self-talk into positive self-talk, you are giving them the gift of self-empowerment. They realize that they have the power to create the life they dream of, and it all starts with believing in yourself.

You may want to try Activity 4 "All About Affirmations" in the Appendix. This will provide you and children an opportunity to shift from negative self-talk to positive affirmations that make you feel good and help you attract the life you desire.

Positive Self-Talk Suggestions

Wealth	Fame/Reputation	Relationship
I am grateful for infinite resources available to me. The Universe provides everything I need in creative ways.	My colleagues see me as a valuable and cooperative team member. My students see me as a helpful and positive role model.	My students collaborate and help each other. I am supported by my colleagues.
Family My school is my second family. We feel connected and supported by one another.	**Health** My students radiate vibrant health. My immune system gets stronger every day. I easily overcome any illness.	**Children/ Creativity** Creativity flows easily and effortlessly in our classroom. The students feel supported and secure in this space.
Knowledge The students easily retain knowledge. We are part of a learning community in which our knowledge always grows.	**Career** I am grateful for my career and love what I do. My students can achieve anything they put their minds to. There are abundant opportunities to grow in this profession.	**Helpful People/ Travel** There are so many teachers and other outside resources that want to help our class. We are supported by the parents and community.

Figure 8.2 This chart gives suggested affirmations for that correlate with all nine areas of the bagua map.

Evidence of a Mindful Shift in Education

Teaching children and adults that their thoughts create their feelings is a powerful tool. It helps everyone to become more aware of the personal power they have to create their reality.

More and more schools are starting to realize that children need to be taught more coping skills in the realm of mindfulness. Mindfulness is self-awareness. It refers to living in the present moment so that you are not worried about the future or stuck in the past. When teachers and students are more mindful, they are living in the now. They can more easily deal with challenging situations as they arise.

The article *Instead of Detention, These Students Get Meditation*, Diane Bloom (2016) reported on Robert. W. Coleman Elementary School, an urban school in Baltimore. They created a meditation room where an instructor guides the students on their yoga mats through a series of breathing exercises.

The Mindful Moment Room, as it is called, is being used lieu of suspensions and detention. Faced with common urban challenges, this space provides students with alternative ways to deal with stress and anger. The room gives students a chance to decompress and teaches them positive coping skills that could otherwise be expressed in more disruptive or destructive ways. The Mindful Moment Room is a new way to approach behavior management, and it offers a life skill that students can carry with them into adulthood.

In another effort to prevent discipline issues, all students at Robert W. Coleman Elementary School start and end their day with a 15-minute guided meditation over the intercom, which is led by the principal.

Tamar Mendelson is an associate professor at the Johns Hopkins Bloomberg School of Public Health, specializing in mental health. Mendelson has been working with the Holistic Life Foundation, which brought the Mindful Moment Room to Coleman. "These kids who are dealing with high-stress situations a lot of the time are coming into school on high alert. Their body's alarm system is switched way on, so they may be primed for fight or flight and are not able to sit calmly and pay attention," Tamar Mendelson commented. "When we sit with pain or discomfort rather than act on it, we learn that feelings and sensations come and go. We don't necessarily need to act on them all. We have a chance to pause and make a thoughtful choice about how to respond," (Bloom, 2016, p.4).

Educators can share simple techniques such as diaphragmatic breathing, or "belly breathing" to help students deal with anxiety. Diaphragmatic breathing is said to be the body's most natural way of breathing. When you inhale, the stomach area rises, and when you exhale the stomach contracts. Breathing consciously can bring about a sense of calm and help to combat stress.

"4-7-8 Breathing" Exercise"

1. Sit up straight.

2. Breathe in through your nose for 4 second and allow your stomach to fill with air.

3. Hold the breath for 7 seconds.

4. Slowly release the breathe out through your mouth for 8 seconds, and allow your stomach to contract.

Figure 8.3 These instructions were inspired by the video "4-7-8 Breathing Exercise from Go Zen."

Embracing Mindfulness Every Day

In schools, and even in major league baseball, there is evidence that people are shifting their awareness and more open to embracing mindfulness. Joe Maddon coached the Chicago Cubs into their first World Series championship in over 108 years in 2016.

"Joe is a person that meditates and understands the competitive advantage that meditation has," Darnell McDonald, the Mental Skills Coordinator for the Cubs, told Yoga Journal Live (2014). He explained how meditation and simply being present gives players a competitive edge. "You learn when you get to professional baseball that everyone is good. The separator is the seventh game of the

World Series, the team that is able to execute under pressure, take off the autopilot button," he says, "Everything we do, we do *better* in the present moment.

Joe Maddon was able to lead the Cubs to their first World Series win in 108 years by teaching them to be in the present moment. Imagine what miracles will come to you and your students by being present this year. It is never too late to start practicing mindfulness or change your course.

If mindfulness can help the Chicago Cubs break the 108-year Curse of the Billy Goat, and it can reduce Robert W. Coleman's suspensions from four in 2014 to zero in 2016, then it is worth considering introducing belly breathing, meditation, or other mindfulness concepts to teachers and students.

Part III
Feng Shui Your Home

Chapter 9
Creating a Sanctuary

"Everything around you is calling to you; everything is telling you a story. Make sure it's a good one."
-J.C. Purr

For optimal results, teachers or anyone else looking to improve their career should try feng shui in their homes too. No matter how neat and organized your classroom or office is, if you are coming home to disarray, you will not feel rejuvenated for the next day. You should feel like your house is giving you a big warm hug every time you walk through the door. If you have a strong foundation at home, your professional life will naturally start to fall into place.

You want your home to be a place of refuge-- safe and tranquil, away from the hustle bustle of the outside world. If this is not your current situation, there is still hope! You have the ability to transform the energy of your home almost instantly.

When we tried to sell our first house, it sold in less than three days. We had four offers over asking price. Of course there were many factors that contributed to the sale such as timing, home staging, and listing it at fair market value. However, the buyers also wanted our home because it *felt* good once they walked in. That's the power of feng shui. Feng shui not only addresses the aesthetic appeal of your home, but it also improves the invisible energy that everyone can feel instantly upon entering your space.

As we looked for our next house, there were many times that the pictures online *looked* great, but when we got into the house, it did not *feel* great. You can hide blemishes on the walls of your home, but you cannot hide its energy. Energy can be felt by everyone, at any time.

You can improve the energy of your home with feng shui so that visitors feel good, and so you feel uplifted after spending time there. Your home should, and can, inspire you and recharge you for the next day.

Have you ever considered your home as a part of your family? Have you ever talked to it-- thanked it for keeping you safe? This chapter will not only give you ideas on how to decorate your home, but it will encourage you to see your home from a whole new perspective. You will see your home as a representation of your life, and you will start to see that each space carries a special energetic vibration that will either support or hinder you.

The good news is that you have the power to influence the energy in *all* areas of your life *and* your home. So buckle up; it's going to be a fun and exciting journey!

How to Use Part III

Have you been trying to apply feng shui in your home but things still feel off? Are you struggling to get unstuck in some areas of your life? Perhaps you have not addressed some of the most important areas of your home. If you focus on the entranceway, kitchen, and master bedroom, you will feel an impact almost immediately.

You may not realize that a bathroom could be significantly affecting the flow of chi in certain areas of your life. The bathrooms are the least energy-enhancing spaces. A bathroom drains energy wherever it is. You will get tips on how to keep the bathroom energy from "draining the life" out of whichever gua it is located in.

The following chapters will take you through your own personal consultation of the most important spaces in your home. Each chapter explains the significance of each space. You will learn how to balance yin and yang; understand the impact of clutter; and start to address common problems associated with each area.

At the end of each chapter there is a checklist to summarize the feng shui suggestions. You can reference these checklists as you apply feng shui principles to the most important areas of your home. Happy feng shui-ing!

Chapter 10

The Main Entrance

"Exterior movement creates interior shift."
-Laurie Pawli

Before making any changes to your front door, ask yourself, "How often do I use it?" You might be surprised to realize how rarely you use the main entrance, especially if you usually go through a garage door. Even if this is not the case, it is important to understand why using your front door every single day is important.

The front door is considered the "mouth of chi." It nourishes your home each time it opens. The front entrance is the first impression that you, your guests, and potential homebuyers see, so you want it to be captivating. When you open the door and welcome in guests, they bring in their personal chi. You can embrace all good chi by making the exterior and interior entryways welcoming.

The Front Door: Yin or Yang?

Although all areas of the home benefit from a balance of yin and yang, some areas need softer, more relaxing energetic representation, while others relish in exuberant colors and vibrant energy. You want your front door to stand out, so the best way to do this is by incorporating colors and elements that constitute *yang* energy.

You want the front door to stand out so that all of the fresh chi can find its way to your doorstep. You can draw attention to your front door by painting it a bright color. If you prefer a neutral door, you can still make it stand out by adding a colorful wreath or pots of bright flowers on the doorstep.

The Importance of Decluttering Your Entranceway

Are there old newspapers or dead flowers on your front door stoop? Are there cobwebs or dried leaves and dirt gathered in the corners? You want to make your door as welcoming as possible. When you sweep your front porch and declutter it, you are clearing a space for fresh new opportunities to come your way.

Since everyone brings their own personal chi through the door upon entering, you want to make the pathway to your house as pleasant as possible to get the good vibes going. A winding sidewalk up to the entrance is most auspicious, or favorable, because it allows the chi to flow smoothly to your house. You may want to line the sidewalk with lights so that the pathway to your home is visible at night as well. By making these exterior adjustments, you will *feel* a difference almost immediately.

Home maintenance and household repairs are part of the fundamental principles of feng shui. Make sure the doorbell is in working condition and the porch lights are all functioning. You do not want any people, packages, or opportunities to "pass you by."

When you walk up to the front door, is your path obstructed in any way? Trim bushes and tree branches so that anyone can easily access your front door. All of these little fixes can make a big difference and elevate the energy of your entire home.

Three Common Front Door Dilemmas

There are three common predicaments that people run into with their front door, but do not fret. In feng shui, there is always a cure! Three common problems are: staircase across from the front door; living across the street from too much or too little activity; or living in a number 4 house. If you find yourself in any of these scenarios,

Staircase Across from the Front Door

you can apply the feng shui adjustments to improve the energy of your home.

Upon entering a home, it is very common for there to be a staircase across from the front door. The energy could rush up the staircase too quickly to the lower, or the higher floor, instead of nourishing the entryway and the rest of the house. In addition, the staircase could push the good energy back out the door.

Solution: Place a round rug on the floor of the interior entrance to circulate the chi more evenly. If you have a light in the foyer, place a feng shui crystal in the light, or hang it with a nine-inch red thread. The crystal will disperse the chi more evenly each time the door opens.

Living Across the Street from Too Much or Too Little Activity

Problem	Solution
You live across the street from a church or a cemetery. If the church is often vacant or hosts a lot of funerals, it could have a depressing effect on your home. Plus, often people go there to pray about many problems which also drains energy. Cemeteries are very quiet and therefore have very "yin" energy. It is believed health problems or mental anguish could plague the residents of homes near cemeteries.	A good protection and blessing cure is to place a bagua mirror over the front door on the outside. The bagua mirror is only to be used outside of the house to reflect back negative engery (sha chi) that is pointing at your home.

You live on a busy road or at a "T" intersection. The chi rushes towards your home and could destroy your goals and possibly your family's health, relationship and fortune. It is advisable to avoid living at a "T" in the road, but if you are in this situation you can protect your house.	A solid front door is ideal. If you have a window on your door, cover it with a wreath or a decorative item that brings you joy. Consider painting the door red or placing pots of red flowers outside to block the chi that is rushing towards your house.
You live in a cul-de-sac or "dead end". Cul-de-sacs have a lot of yin energy because the energy slows down as it circulates. Streets with "no outlet" stop the energy from flowing around your house, which also limits the potential of residents.	To liven up the entrance of your home, place a wind chime to circulate the chi. You could also add a fountain in front of your home to keep the energy flowing.

Figure 10.1

Living in a Number 4 House

If you add the numbers of your home, does it equal 4? My mom lived in a "4 House," 14062.

$$1+4+0+6+2= 13$$
$$1+3=4$$

Although the number 4 is associated with money in feng shui, it is also sounds like the word "death" in Chinese. Therefore, a number "4" house is not an auspicious number.

Solution: You can energetically change a 4 house. The best addresses add up to 3, 8, or 9.

3 represents the circle of energy and balance and sounds like "growth" in Chinese

8 represents abundance and infinite possibilities and sounds like "prosperity"

9 is the most energetic, powerful number and sounds like "forever or long-lasting"

To energetically change the address "14062", I took a red pen and changed the "4" to an "8" and said a feng shui mantra to seal my intention. The new numbers added up to "8". Within three months she found herself in a much better financial situation with more security and peace of mind.

$$1+\underline{8}+0+6+2= 17$$
$$1+7=8$$

There are some feng shui practitioners and numerologists that would say that the number of your house is not as important as the energy of the people who live in the home. So even if your house number is not what you want it to be, know that you can still attract all good things into your life by nourishing your personal chi and applying feng shui throughout the whole house.

Front Door Checklist

- **Place a solid doormat on the outside of your door:** It will help you welcome new opportunities into your home. Make sure the mat is the same size or smaller than the door. Although it may sound like a good thing, an oversized doormat could send an overabundance of opportunities that could be too much to handle and wear you out. If you live in an apartment and cannot place a mat outside your door, you can "draw" an imaginary mat with red marker and write your intentions and the opportunities you wish to attract to your front door.

Teaching from the Heart with Feng Shui

- **Place a wind chime outside of your door:** The wind chime will keep the positive chi flowing.
- **Avoid placing a mirror directly across from your door in the foyer:** You want to welcome positive chi into your home, and a mirror will reflect the good energy back out the door.
- **Have your address clearly labeled on your door:** You want people to be able to find you, and you want all the mail and packages to get to you easily. I added this to our home and I felt a difference immediately. More guests and helpful people started coming around, and it made the porch look nicer too.

Chapter 11
The Master Bedroom

"When you want something,
all the Universe conspires in helping you to achieve it."
–Paulo Coelho, The Alchemist

The master bedroom is one of the most important rooms in the house. If you are new to feng shui, the master bedroom is a great place to start. You spend nearly one third of your time in your bedroom because it is where you sleep. When you apply adjustments to your bedroom, you will experience improvements in *all* areas of your life no matter which gua your master bedroom is located.

Bedrooms: Yin or Yang?

When applying feng shui to the master bedroom, your goal is to attract the Three R's: rest, rejuvenation, and romance. In order to achieve these results, you will need a healthy balance of yin and yang, and you will want to make all changes with this intention in mind.

For a restful night sleep you will want to have a majority of *yin* color and texture representation. Avoid bright wall colors such as red, purple or fuchsia which will promote alertness. Even sky blue is not very desirable for the bedroom. Blue represents the Water element which is always in motion. It could cause you to feel overly emotional and unrestful. You can also represent *yin* energy with soft pillows, comforters and textures, as well as soft lighting.

In order to achieve harmony in your bedroom, you should add some *yang* accents so that the room does not feel too monotone or underwhelming. The fire element is very active, so lighting a candle will bring exuberance to the space. You might add some red accent pillows or a piece of romantic artwork with bright colors. These *yang* representations are important to keep your room feeling vibrant when you want to add romance and excitement into your life.

The Importance of Decluttering Your Bedroom

Like all rooms in your house, clutter in the bedroom can hinder your clarity and cause anxiety. It is especially important to clean and minimize the objects in your bedroom so that you feel peaceful throughout the night while you recharge for the next day.

Have you kept your treadmill or a desk in your bedroom? This is clutter! Your bedroom should promote relaxation. Exercising and paying bills at a desk in your bedroom is far from relaxing. Try to find another room to place these objects, or donate them if they have been unused in the past year.

The most important space to declutter is under your bed. There should be nothing under your bed so that the chi can circulate around you as you sleep. The circulation of chi is what provides you with a satisfying night of sleep.

The condition of your room is a reflection of your mind. Clear the clutter from your night stands and closets. Get rid of old clothing that you never wear. If you change your environment, you can change the way you feel. This knowledge will change your life!

Three Common Bedroom Dilemmas

The master bedroom is among the most important areas to feng shui. Throughout my feng shui consultation experiences, and from my own personal experiences, I have encountered many common predicaments when arranging bedroom furniture. The three most common challenges are: no space for two nightstands; obstacles placing the bed in the power position; and slanted ceilings. This section explains how to address all three challenges.

No Space for Two Nightstands

It is ideal to place a nightstand on both sides of the bed with matching or similar-sized lamps. This promotes equality in a relationship and more opportunities to see eye-to-eye.

Only having one nightstand is not desirable because the partner with the light and table could have more power in the relationship. The other partner may feel less important or undervalued. Even if you are single, you should have two nightstands to welcome a partner into your life and promote balance in your personal life.

Solution: If you do not have enough space, even for two small tables, you could put a floor lamp on both sides of the bed. Another option is to hang a wall sconce on each side of the bed. This way each side is lit equally.

If you only have one end table, do not place it next to the bed. Find another space for it in the room so that the bed is symmetrical and promotes harmony.

Who has the power in your house?

Did you know that the master bedroom should be located in the wealth or relationship gua? These areas are considered the "power positions" of the household. If children occupy these areas, and a parent's bedroom does not, this could be a dilemma for the household. The children will have more power in the family and call the shots. In order to fix this, you could place a mirror in the wealth or relationship gua; make sure it is facing the master bedroom. This will energetically pull the master bedroom into a power position and create more balance in the family.

Placing the Bed in the Power Position

It is particularly critical to have the bed in good placement, yet very few bedrooms have the dimensions and architectural configurations to perfectly accommodate a feng shui bedroom. Before addressing some of the common challenges, you must first know the ideal power position.

Solution: There are a lot of guidelines in order to place your bed in the power position. With such specific criteria, it is easy to see how one might run into obstacles when trying to apply the best placement. Figure 11.2 gives a list of three common challenges and how to address them.

How to Place Your Bed in the Power Position

- Place the bed against a solid wall to provide support and a "mountain behind you."
- When you lay down, you want to be able to see the door. However, you do not want your feet directly in line with the door, as it will drain your energy.
- Make the bed accessible from both sides. If you push your bed against the wall, one person could feel "trapped" in the relationship. If you are looking for a relationship, you should still keep your bed accessible from both sides. This sets the intention that you are welcoming someone else into your life.

Figure 11.1

Common Challenges of Placing the Bed in the Power Position

Problem	Solution
Your bed has a window behind it. It is best to have a solid wall behind the bed to act a "mountain" which promotes security and support while you sleep.	Every bed should have a solid headboard to create a "mountain" behind you for stability. Therefore, it is even *more* vital to invest in a solid headboard if your bed is against a window. In addition to blinds, get some curtains that you can draw each night for additional window coverage. Place a multi-faceted feng shui crystal on the windowsill to disperse any active energy from the outside.
Your feet point towards the entrance or are in line with a bathroom. If your body is in line with a door, the chi could affect your sleep and even cause body aches.	Place a piece of red electrical tape on the inside of the bed frame in line with where the door is located. The red tape acts as a stopper, and it will slow the chi down from "hitting" your body.
You cannot see the entrance of the room from where you are. It is believed that when you can see the entrance of the room you will sleep more securely. Knowing that nobody will sneak up on you at night gives you greater peace of mind.	If your bed must be positioned in such a way that you cannot see the door, you could add a small mirror to the room so that you can see the door from where you sleep. Although mirrors are not generally recommended in the bedroom because of their *yang* presence, this is an exception.

Figure 11.2

Slanted Ceilings

Although sloped ceilings in the bedroom might look like a nice architectural personalization, they are not ideal for a feng shui bedroom. The ceiling creates a kind of downward pressure that affects your sleep patterns which could lead to health problems.

Solutions: Do not place your bed under the slanted ceiling. This could leave you feeling constricted and cause restlessness.

1. Place the bed so that the headboard is under the highest part of the slope which will give you a sense of expansion. Placing it against a solid wall is always important, but in this case it is vital.

2. Paint the slanted ceiling a uniform color. Since it is in the bedroom, the colors should be skin-toned or neutral.

3. Draw attention away from the sloped ceiling. For example, you could place a piece of artwork on the wall without the slant. Choose a piece with uplifting colors or positive quotes to attract attention.

Master Bedroom Checklist

- **Only place pictures that promote romance:**

    ○ The bedroom is not the place to put all of your family photos and pictures of your children. Doing this welcomes other people's energy into your love life. Hang happy, recent pictures of you and your partner (no older than one year). The best pictures are of the two of you looking into each other's eyes.

    ○ Keep the painting of a solo woman gazing at the beach somewhere else. You will attract into your life that which you surround yourself with. Take advantage of this

- knowledge by incorporating images of things you want to manifest into your life and place them strategically throughout your home.

    ○ Any décor using pairs will attract more romance into your life. For example, a picture of two red flowers or two birds would be great. You can place the bagua map on your entire master bedroom and you can activate any area of your life. For example, when you enter the bedroom, the relationship area is in the upper right hand corner. You could place a pair of objects or artwork in that corner to activate the romance in your relationship.

- **Avoid mirrors and water elements:** Mirrors could cause unrest because they continually more the energy. Water is always moving and flowing, which could also cause unrest or cause you to feel over-emotional.

- **Ditch the TV:** Having the TV in the bedroom hinders you from focusing on your partner. It's *yang* energy could keep you restless at night. As if that wasn't enough, the TV "invites a third party" into your bedroom and your relationship. If you must have a TV, invest in a decorative cabinet so that you can close the doors and hide it at night.

- **Energetically fix the ceiling fan:** It is very common to have a ceiling fan above your bed. However, a ceiling fan will cut the chi and could lead to unrest. In order to address this problem, place a small red dot on the top of each ceiling fan blade. The red dot acts a stopper and prevents the energy from cutting into your energy field.

- **Have a solid headboard:** Do you have a headboard? It creates a "mountain" behind you, which will make you feel more stable and secure. A solid headboard will provide the best energetic support. It could be wooden or cloth. Metal headboards are really only ideal for psychics and clairvoyants. Metal promotes communication and activity, so it will not give you the most restful sleep.

Ready to Feng Shui!

You might want to refer to Activity 6 in the Appendix, "Feng Shui Your Bedroom." It will give you the chance to plan how to rearrange your furniture if necessary. You will learn how to place your bed in the best power position for your space. You will also see which areas of your bedroom represents specific areas of your life. Engaging in this activity will give you a chance to reflect on the current color schemes and decorations that you have, so that you can make improvements to your space and feel the results almost instantly!

Chapter 12
The Kitchen

"Use your good stuff."
-Oprah

The kitchen represents the nourishment of your home and the abundance of your life. The kitchen is the place where you cook and nurture the ones you love. Have you ever noticed that guests generally gather in the kitchen? It is the nucleus of the home. When your kitchen is in order, many other areas of your life will fall into place; this is why a good feng shui kitchen is essential.

The Kitchen: Yin or Yang?

Like all areas of the home, a healthy balance of yin and yang is encouraged in the kitchen. However, the kitchen is overall a lively space that benefits from light, fire, and vibrant *yang* energy!

In fact, the kitchen is the "fire energy" room. The stove is the main appliance that generates a flow of abundance because the fire energy enters the kitchen space through the burners and brings with it the chi that draws in prosperity.

White cabinets and white quartz or granite countertops are all very popular features in kitchens right now. The color white represents *yang* qualities, which is great for a kitchen. A kitchen with a lot of dark tones will carry mostly *yin* energy. You could add *yang* by painting the walls or kitchen cabinets a lighter color which would also produce a more balanced look.

You can add subtle *yin* representations to kitchens to promote balance. Accent decor with dark colors or dim lighting have softer, *yin* energy. An oil-rubbed bronze light fixture in a mostly-white kitchen could create an elegant, harmonious look. Adding a dimmer switch, pendant lights, or a small accent lamp could also soften up the kitchen.

The most important thing to consider when evaluating the yin and yang characteristics of your kitchen is how you *feel* when you are in the space. Does it lift your spirits or make you feel drained? The more you love your kitchen, the better you will feel when cooking. In feng shui it is believed that your feelings transfer into the food you cook. So bring on the beauty, and bring out the joy!

The Importance of Decluttering Your Kitchen

Clutter and uncleanliness in the kitchen can affect the health and well-being of all residents. Since the kitchen is thought to represent abundance, it is very important for it to be clean and welcoming.

A well-stocked pantry and refrigerator are good feng shui symbols of wealth. Keep your wealth clean and flowing by dedicating one day a week to go through the refrigerator to get rid of old, outdated food. Toss leftovers after a couple days, and look at the expiration dates on condiments. Getting rid of the old will make room for the new.

When it comes to keeping the kitchen clean, make the stove a priority! The stove oversees your finances and brings in prosperity chi. Problems with the stove could mean problems with your wealth.

Make sure the stove is clean before you cook your meals. You can lay the bagua map on the stove burners and see which burner represents certain areas of life and activate accordingly. You want to use all of the burners throughout the week so that you are initiating abundance in all areas such as wealth, relationships, wisdom, and helpful people. Rotating the burners will keep your finances working in your favor.

Three Common Kitchen Dilemmas

The kitchen is an extremely important room in your house. Unfortunately, we do not have a lot of control over where it is located or where the appliances are located. The three major challenges people run into when trying to feng shui their kitchen are: the kitchen is visible upon entering the home, the stove is towards the front of the house, and the sink and stove are across from each other. All of these are permanent structural issues that are difficult to change, but do not fret. In feng shui there is always a cure!

The Kitchen is Visible Upon Entering the Home

If the kitchen is the first thing you see when you enter your home, you could struggle with your weight.

Solutions:

The first solution is awareness. When you realize that entering through the kitchen could cause cravings and overeating, you can use this knowledge to make more conscious decisions.

Another option is to enter through another door, if possible. However, the front door is very important and should still be used at least once a day.

A third suggestion is to place a large, eye-catching piece of artwork on a wall away from the kitchen. This could draw your attention away from the kitchen upon entering your home.

The Stove is Towards the Front of the Home

The farther to the back of the house that the stove is, the better! Since the stove represents the wealth in your home, it is more secure the further back it is. If you can see the stove from the front door, then you could be losing opportunities. Additionally, your finances could be transparent to others.

Solutions:

You can energetically pull the stove back by placing a mirror in the back of the house, and reflect the stove in the mirror. If people can see your stove from the front door, try hanging a bright picture or eye-catching quote nearby or above the stove. This could distract people from looking at the stove and meddling in your finances.

The Sink is Across from the Stove

If the sink is across from the stove, the water energy of the sink will drain the fire energy of the stove. You don't want your abundance to be drained by the sink!

Solution:

Try placing a red sink mat on the floor between the sink and the oven. The red will stop the sink from draining energy from the stove. You might also consider lighting a candle by the sink frequently.

Kitchen Checklist

- **Sit at your dining room table at least once a day:** Many people eat at a kitchen island if they have one, and some people even eat on their couch. The dining room table (or kitchen table if you do not have a dining room), represents the abundance in your home. Try to sit there at least once a day, even if it is just for a cup of coffee or to check your e-mail. Sitting at the dining room table represents your openness to receiving all the goodness that the universe has to offer. Soak it in!

- **Place a mirror facing your dining room table:** Reflecting the dining room table with a mirror will expand it and multiply the abundance exponentially. Additionally, the mirror represents water and money. The dining room is a great place to symbolize money flowing into your home.

- **Keep the refrigerator full:** If you live alone, you might find that you do not need that much food in your refrigerator. A solution is to keep a couple gallons of water in the fridge to fill the space. This also saves energy since the refrigerator functions better when it is full.

- **Add a bowl of fresh fruit on the counter or table:** Place a mirror face up underneath the bowl of fruit to symbolize multiplying abundance. Oranges represent wealth in feng shui, so that would be a great choice. The number nine is the most energetic number in feng shui, so that would be an ideal number to put in a bowl. If you have trouble keeping the fruit fresh, it would be better to use artificial fruit that looks real. Real fruit and flowers are always best, but something artificial that looks real is better than displaying something that is rotting.

- **Keep a vase of fresh flowers in the kitchen or at the dining room table:** Flowers soak up negative chi and give off positive energy, much like crystals. They add life and vibrancy to the space. Since it can be difficult to keep up with fresh flowers weekly, bamboo or mini bonsai trees are a great way to add life to the kitchen.

- **Take knives off the countertops:** Knives cut the chi and can be unsettling to look at. As a feng shui consultant, I knew this information, however, it took me a while to remove the convenient block of knives off the counter. One day I finally tried it. I simply placed the knives in a drawer and stored the empty block in the closet. Doing this gave me so much more peace of mind, and I enjoyed the extra counter space! If you ever doubt these suggestions, I would recommend trying them for a week. If you don't like it, you can always put it back the way it was.

Chapter 13
Uplifting the Bathrooms

*"Every single thing we made on this
planet started with imagination.
Begin to imagine your new life."*
-Bryant Mcgill

The bathrooms are considered the least energetic. The drains of the shower, bathtub, sink, and toilet drain the energy. If you lay the bagua map on your floor plan, you can see which areas of your life could be feeling drained because a bathroom is in that space.

If a bathroom is in the wealth area, you might find that you frequently feel like you are throwing money away or spending it carelessly. If there is a bathroom in the knowledge gua, you might find that you have had challenges thinking clearly and making wise decisions. A bathroom in the children and creativity space could mean that your children are struggling in school or that you are having difficulty conceiving.

There are some things that you can do to slow down the draining energy of the bathroom. This chapter will give you ideas on how to add the Earth and fire elements to the bathroom to counteract the water element and strengthen specific areas of your life. If you still do not see improvements after applying these tips, you may want to consider hiring a feng shui consultant to conduct a professional "Sealing of the Toilets" ceremony.

The Bathroom: Yin or Yang?

The bathroom is a space that could benefit from a lot of *yang* energy. Bright colors and candles represent fire, and this could keep the bathroom from being so parasitic!

When selecting colors for the bathroom, your main priority should be avoiding colors that represent water, since the bathroom already has so much water representation. Avoid a lot of blue and black and any wavy or odd-shaped decorations. If your bathroom is already painted blue, you may consider adding some Earth or fire elements for balance.

The Importance of Decluttering Your Bathroom

Although the bathroom is not a favored space, it should still not be neglected. Clearing clutter in the bathroom is a must. If you feel overwhelmed or disgusted when you enter the bathroom, that feeling will only be magnified by all of the drains in the bathroom, leaving you feeling depleted.

Keep the cabinets organized so that you feel better in the space. Letting go of outdated healthcare products or unused hair accessories keeps the flow of giving and receiving in balance. You must let go of the old in order to welcome the new.

Three Common Bathroom Dilemmas

Although the bathroom has low energy, it is still very important that you like being in the space. If you have been putting off a bathroom remodel, perhaps you will reconsider procrastinating after reading this chapter. In the meantime, there are three common bathroom dilemmas that you can address: plumbing issues, the toilet seat, and unattractive décor.

Plumbing Issues

Make sure if the plumbing needs repairs that you tend to those matters immediately. The plumbing systems in your house represent money and emotions. When plumbing issues arise, it is time to take a close look at your personal life and what your home is telling you.

Is the toilet constantly running? Perhaps you've been "flushing money down the drain." Is the shower drain clogged? Maybe you have been unwilling to share your wealth or let go of objects that no longer serve you. Making sure the plumbing is in working order could help you address some of the emotional and financial issues that you have been battling.

The Toilet Seat is Always Up!

It is important to keep the toilet seats down. When toilets are flushed, they draw an enormous amount of chi down the drain. You might even consider keeping the bathtub and sink drains closed when not in use.

Unattractive Decor

Since the bathrooms are so draining, it is important that you make them look beautiful. A well designed space will make you feel good. These emotions will radiate the room and boost the chi around you. This is especially important around drains.

If your faucets or other hardware are broken, mismatched or outdated, you are not maximizing the chi in your space. They are likely creating stagnant energy that will hinder growth in all areas of your life. So, if you have been putting off a bathroom remodel for a long time, perhaps you might consider moving it back up to the top of your list.

Bathroom Checklist

- **Put live plants in the bathroom.** You could place a bamboo plant on top of the toilet. Since the bamboo is tall and sturdy, it counteracts the draining energy of the toilet. Live plants in general are energy boosters. Placing plants in the bathroom will slow the energy down, clean the air, and balance the elements.

- **Add the Earth element to soak up the water element.** The Earth Element is represented with the shape of a square, flowers, or the colors of Earth (yellow, sand colors, or beige). Examples of Earth representation could be a square photo of flowers, yellow hand towels, or a dish of decorative shells or rocks.

- **Apply the fire element to counteract the water element.** The fire element is represented by the shape of a triangle, candles, or the colors of fire (red or bright orange). An example of applying the fire element would be adding red hand towels or a red shower curtain. You could also place a candle, especially if you are not a fan of the fire colors. Even when the candle is unlit, it still represents the fire energy.

- **Keep the toilet seat down.** This will slow down the draining energy.

- **Close the bathroom door at night if it is attached to your bedroom.** This will protect and strengthen your personal chi.

Chapter 14
Feng Shui for Kids

*"My definition of beautiful
is a space where you can be yourself to the fullest."*
-Xorin Balbes

Just as it is vital for teachers and parents to feel rejuvenated at home, the energy of *every* room also affects children. Applying feng shui to children's bedrooms can help them sleep and concentrate better.

Kids Bedroom: Yin or Yang?

Just like the master bedroom, a child's bedroom should be predominantly *yin* energy. The *yin* qualities promote quietness, softness, and relaxation. You want to set up your child's bedroom so that she feels restful in the space.

Depending on the layout of your house, you may have tried to make your child's bedroom a playroom and a study area as well. These areas would require more *yang* representation to promote alertness and attentiveness. This contradicts the mood that you want to set for your child at bedtime.

In order to create the most tranquil environment, it is best to set your child's bedroom up for a singular purpose: sleep. Keep the toys, games, and study nook out of sight from your child's bed, so that she can get the most rejuvenating rest.

Although bright pink and bright blue are popular paint colors for children's rooms, neither one is ideal. Pink represents the fire element, which possesses active *yang* energy. Blue represents the water element, which will increase emotions and could cause restlessness. However, you may choose *pastel* tones of pink, blue, and green because they are softer and more soothing.

Busy patterns on the wall such as stripes or floral wall paper will also increase the *yang* energy and could be overstimulating. These designs would be more fitting for a playroom or basement where the children are encouraged to be active and creative.

Of course, life is all about balance. If you really want an accent wall in the nursery, just make sure the bedding and other accent decor patterns are subtle. If your child really likes a particular bedspread with vibrant colors, make sure the room is painted more *yin*, or soft tones. Children's bedrooms are really all about them. Giving them the freedom to make design choices that represent their style and personality will make them feel empowered and develop their self-confidence and personal identity.

The Importance of Decluttering Kid's Rooms

The best way to create a clutter-free environment in a kid's room is to have attractive storage boxes, drawers and shelves. If the toys and games can be organized and concealed before bedtime, it will promote a much more relaxing sleep.

Since children are very sensitive to energy, it is important for the room to be clutter-free at the end of the day. Encourage them to help put their toys away because being surrounded by a messy playground of activity is not conducive to a peaceful night of rest.

Three Common Children's Room Dilemmas

A Child's Room is Out of the Bagua

If a child's room falls outside of the bagua map on your floor plan, that child may feel "left out" of the family and very often misunderstood. To find out if your child's room is outside of the bagua map, follow the guidelines in Figure 14.1.

How to Lay the Bagua on the Second Floor
1. The main entrance or the "front door" to the second floor of your home is where you enter from the stairs.
2. Position the bagua map on the stairs, where you enter the second floor. You will be entering in the knowledge, career, or helpful people gua.
3. If there are bedrooms behind the stairway, they are left out of the bagua map for the second floor.

Figure 14.1

Solution:

If a child's room is outside of the bagua map, hang a mirror on a wall within the bagua map, and face the mirror towards the bedroom that is not within the bagua. This will energetically draw the bedroom into the bagua, and your child will feel more included in the family.

If you are unable to hang a mirror on the wall, you could place a decoration with reflective, mirror-like properties in a space within the bagua. Make sure the decor reflects the bedroom door so that it will energetically pull the bedroom back into the bagua map.

Please note that if the master bedroom is out of the bagua, you would also want to apply this creative solution so that the parents have power and inclusion in the family.

Child's Room is Across from the Stairs

If the child's bedroom door is directly across from a flight of stairs, this could cause anxiety, restlessness, and even illness. The chi either rushes up into the bedroom, or the stairs drain the chi from it.

Solution:

Make sure the child's bed is not in line with the door. Place a feng shui crystal above the door to disperse the chi more evenly. You could also apply this cure if the master bedroom is across from stairs.

Child's Bedroom Door is Across from a Bathroom

If the bathroom is directly across from a bedroom, it will drain the energy of the occupants and the gua.

Solution:

Place a crystal above the bedroom door. My daughter's bedroom was across from the bathroom, so I placed a crystal on the ledge on the outside of her bedroom door. The purpose was also to protect her energy. Her bedroom was located in the career gua. By placing the crystal, the intention was also to protect our careers from being draining or from getting drained by the energy of the bathroom.

Kid's Room Checklist

- **Incorporate happy family photos.** Children love to see pictures of themselves and their family. This promotes a sense of security and well-being.

- **Hang your child's artwork.** It is important that children feel valued. Having a special designated wall for artwork makes them feel seen. It also gives them a sense of ownership of their bedroom.

- **Put the bed in the power position.** (See Chapter 11, Figure 11.1)

- **Include soft lighting.** Soft lighting promotes *yin* energy which makes the room feel more peaceful. Have multiple lamps in addition to overhead lighting to give your child options as to whether they want to promote alertness or relaxation in the room.

Chapter 15
Enjoying Your Feng Shui Home

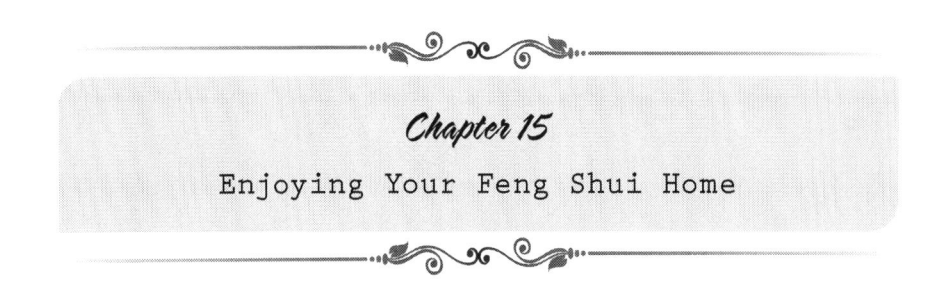

"What you seek is seeking you."
-Rumi

Your home is an affirmation for the life you desire! The best part of feng shui is that you get to design and create your world. You are the creator of the life you wish to experience. If you don't like the way things are going, you have the power to improve your surroundings so that you feel more inspired and uplifted throughout your days.

As you make changes to the major areas of your home, keep in mind that energy loves to move. After you make adjustments, you will need to revisit these spaces to maintain the positive energy; sweep your front porch to revitalize the front door, or move some pictures or decorations around in your bedroom for a new perspective.

Your life is always changing, which means your needs and desires are too. As your life evolves, so should your home. As you apply these changes, you will start to get into your own rhythm and learn how to add your personal style to each area. Have fun and know you cannot go wrong when you have the right intention behind each cure!

Coming Up...

If you stopped reading right here, you would have a pretty good foundation for your feng shui journey. However, I have been living a feng shui lifestyle for a few years now, and I have learned a lot of creative ways to integrate feng shui into day-to-day activities and living.

Part IV will give you more supplies for your feng shui toolbox. You will learn about your personal feng shui element and how to change your environment to support your personal energy and the energy of your loved ones. The next chapter will be particularly helpful for teachers who wish to create a classroom that will nourish the birth elements of the students, which could result in a calmer learning environment.

Part IV
Personalized Feng Shui

Chapter 16
Birth Elements and How They Interact

"Nobody is superior, nobody is inferior, but nobody is equal.
People are simply unique, incomparable.
You are you, and I am I."
-Osho

How is everyone getting along around you? Even if you followed all of the suggestions in the previous chapters, you might still find that the relationships in your home or classroom are unbalanced. Knowing which elements support your family members, or your students, will improve interactions.

Everyone is born under one of the five elements. The concept is similar to astrology, where each of the five elements have certain qualities and characteristics, just as the twelve zodiac signs do.

When I learned that my husband is a fire element and I am a wood element, it was an "ah-ha" moment for me! He possesses a lot of fiery qualities; he is passionate about his family and career, fiercely loyal, and very outspoken. Wood fuels fire, so I motivate my husband. On the other hand, fire burns wood! At times, I could feel overwhelmed by his exuberance and find it difficult to relax. Once I realized it was natural for me to feel this way because of our elements, I knew I had to add more decor to our home to support my energy and our relationship.

In order to feel more supported and less "burnt up" from the fire element, I added decor that represented the Earth element. When you toss dirt on a fire, it reduces it. Adding Earth was easy. I placed yellow accent pillows on the couch, hung square picture frames in the living room, and put a vase of fresh flowers on our kitchen table. Almost immediately I felt much more relaxed and nourished in our home.

When you know your element, you will have a better understanding of your personal characteristics and preferences. You can use the knowledge in this chapter to personalize your home and classroom even more! Once you know the elements of those who live with you, you can create a more comfortable environment for everyone.

Using the Birth Element Chart

Find your feng shui birth element by using the chart below. Remember the Chinese new year falls on a different date, usually in January or February, so make sure you pick the right year depending on where New Year fell on that specific year.

Wood	Fire	Earth	Metal	Water
1-25-1925	2-13-1926	1-23-1928	1-30-1930	2-6-1932
2-14-1934	2-2-1927	2-10-1929	2-17-1931	1-26-1933
1-25-1944	1-24-1936	1-31-1938	2-8-1940	1-15-1942
2-13-1945	2-11-1937	2-19-1939	1-27-1941	2-5-1943
2-3-1954	2-2-1946	2-10-1948	2-17-1950	1-27-1952
1-24-1955	1-22-1947	1-29-1949	2-6-1951	2-14-1953
2-13-1964	2-12-1956	2-18-1958	1-28-1960	2-5-1962
2-2-1965	1-31-1957	2-8-1959	2-15-1961	1-25-1963
1-23-1974	1-21-1966	1-30-1968	2-6-1970	2-15-1972
2-11-1975	2-9-1967	2-17-1969	1-27-1971	2-3-1973
2-2-1984	1-31-1976	2-7-1978	2-16-1980	1-25-1982
2-20-1985	2-18-1977	1-28-1979	2-5-1981	2-13-1983
2-10-1994	2-9-1986	2-17-1988	1-27-1990	2-4-1992
1-31-1995	1-29-1987	2-6-1989	2-15-1991	1-23-1993
1-22-2004	2-19-1996	1-28-1998	2-5-2000	2-12-2002

Teaching from the Heart with Feng Shui

2-9-2005	2-7-1997	2-16-1999	1-24-2001	2-1-2003
1-31-2014	1-29-2006	2-2-2008	2-14-2010	1-23-2012
2-19-2015	2-18-2007	1-26-2009	2-3-2011	2-10-2013
2-10-2024	2-8-2016	2-16- 2018	1-25-2020	2-1-2022
1-29-2025	1-28-2017	2-5-2019	2-12-2021	1-22-2023

Figure 16.1 Retrieved on 4/13/2016 from http://consciouspanda.com/feng-shui-basics/

Example of How to Decipher the Table

I was born on October 8, 1984. The new year for 1984, according to the birth chart, falls on 02-02-1984 (January 2, 1984), which is a wood element year.

This school year, my students were born between the years starting 1-22-2004 (January 22, 2004) and 2-9-2005 (February 9, 2005), and those both happen to be wood element years too.

What Does Your Element Mean?

Now that you know your birth element, you can have a better understanding of your personal qualities as well as those around you. You can use this information to better relate to your loved ones, students, or colleagues. You can also use this information to decorate your home, classroom, and office so that it is personally nourishing for you.

Figure 16.2 explains the qualities of the five elements. It is possible to identify with the characteristics of all of the elements. Depending on the season, day of the week, or time of day, our emotions ebb and flow, as do our personalities. Some days you might feel fiery, and other days you might possess more metal qualities. No matter what, you will most likely have natural tendencies, which are associated with your birth element. Awareness is the key to creating a more nurturing environment for yourself and those around you. Knowing your birth element also helps you recognize how others might deplete you.

Qualities of the Elemental Personalities

Element & Color	Qualities	If you have too much...	If you have too little...
Metal- gray, white, and gold	The element of communication, clarity and vision; Ideal for psychics or clairvoyants; Metal elements are precise and possibly perfectionists	Too much metal can lead to judgment, conflict and withdrawal. You could be too analytical, too cold, or too much of a perfectionist.	You may have trouble creating healthy boundaries. You may feel unfocused or unable to communicate clearly.
Water- blue and black	You are a calm person with a fresh perspective; you're happiest near water; Water elements have great introspection and love meditation and reflection	Too much water leads to confusion, isolation, and lack of focus. You may feel overwhelmed by life. Water excess could lead to feeling depressed.	You may feel tired and anxious, as if drinking a cup of coffee right before trying to fall asleep.
Wood- green and brown	The element of growth and flexibility; You are happy being out in nature, especially in the forest; Wood activities include yoga, journaling, and creative activity	You may feel so loaded with potential energy that you get overstimulated, overwhelmed and moody. You may also feel stuck.	You may be introverted or experience a lack of creativity. Low self-esteem is also thought to be a Wood deficiency.
Fire- red, orange, and violets	Fire elements are passionate and have high energy; Create fast, vibrant changes; Impulsive	You may feel anxious or angry.	Insomnia is thought to be a lack of Fire. You may also lack passion and find yourself surrounded by a lot of unfinished projects.

| Earth- yellow, sand, brown | Earth is the great creative element and holds within it a seed of all the other elements; Happiest in a home where strength and stability reign. | You may feel stuck and heavy. It could lead to stagnation and clutter. | You might feel ungrounded. |

Figure 16.2 This chart was inspired by *Feng Shui 101* by Dana Claudat (2013) and *Feng Shui: Create Health, Wealth, and Happiness Through the Power of Your Home* by Davina Mackail (2016). It can serve as an ongoing reference to help you achieve more balance in your environment and within.

How to Support Your Birth Element

Each element is represented by different colors, shapes, images, and the actual element itself. Surrounding yourself with more colors that nourish your birth element will naturally make you feel more energetic, productive, and empowered. Use the Figure 16.3 to apply the elemental cures that will make you feel more secure and help you create a more productive environment.

How to Support the Elements

Your Birth Element	Nourish Your Birth Element With...	Shape & Colors of Supporting Element	Suggested Decorations of Supportive Element
Wood	Water	Element: water Shape: wavy/odd Colors: blue, black	Pictures of the ocean, fish tank, water fountain, thunderstorm or ocean sounds, mirrors
Fire	Wood	Element: wood Shape: vertical rectangle Colors: green, gold, or purple	Rectangular frames (vertical), wooden sculptures or dishes, wood furniture, bamboo plant, money tree, bonsai tree
Earth	Fire	Element: fire Shape: triangle Colors: red, bright orange	Candles, fireplace, picture with reds or bright orange, triangular patterns
Metal	Earth	Element: Earth Shape: square or horizontal rectangle Colors: blue, green, or Earth tones	Square or rectangular (horizontal) picture frames, yellow throw blanket or accent pillows, sand colored towels, sand or rocks in a square dish, a salt lamp, fresh flowers or fake flowers that look real
Water	Metal	Element: metal Shape: circle Colors: white, bright and pastel colors, gray	Metal dishes, coins, circular frames or clocks,, metallic artwork, gray or white throw pillows or curtains

Figure 16.3

Birth Elements in the Classroom

The birth element is based on your birth year. Therefore, each new school year your students will most likely be the same element, depending on which year they were born. Every year, you can prepare for your new class by enhancing the classroom to support their feng shui birth element.

Harnessing Your Personal Feng Shui

You are now on your way to completely personalizing your home, office, or classroom to fit your personal energetic needs. Now that you know your element, you can wear colors that harness your personal energy and bring out the best in you. Did you know that foods represent different elements too? There are so many ways to support your personal energy!

The most important thing to remember when it comes to the elements is that balance is key. In order to feel harmonious, you need a healthy balance of all five elements. Therefore, no element is off-limits for you, regardless of your birth chart. Knowing your birth element helps you to realize your natural tendencies. However, you can possess the qualities of all the elements at any given time and enhance those characteristics depending on your current needs and circumstances.

Chapter 17
Discover Your Personal Direction

"World peace begins with inner peace."
-Dalai Lama

We all have challenges or stressful encounters in our life. The more self-aware we are of our personal energy and of the energy around us, the better we become at avoiding these stumbling blocks. For this reason, it is good to know your "best direction."

We all have four directions that help us achieve optimum success, health, relationships, and personal development. This chapter will help you know which direction is best for you, your loved ones, and your students. Knowing your "best direction" will also increase productivity.

Grand Duke Jupiter

Regardless of your personal direction, everyone needs to be aware of the Duke of Jupiter whose direction changes every year. The Grand Duke Jupiter is one of the most highly respected and feared deities in the Chinese beliefs. In order to have a good and peaceful year, you need to avoid confrontation with the Duke.

According to Chinese mythology, the Grand Duke Jupiter, also known as Tai Sui, is a position in the celestial heavens, which is in charge of the world's affairs for a particular year. A person's happiness, health, luck, and fortune are all under his watchful eye. This position rotates and changes every year in 60 year cycles.

How does this impact your year? You should avoid facing the direction of the Grand Duke each year to avoid confrontation. It is greatly recommended to take precautions not to disturb him throughout the year. An offended Tai Sui will cause misfortunes, from mild to severe.

A Personal Clash with the Grand Duke Jupiter

In 2017 The Grand Duke resided in the West. As my husband and I prepared to put our house on the market, we needed to make some improvements to a foundational crack on the west side of our house. This was not a very ideal adjustment to make since it could upset the Grand Duke, but we did it anyway since we did not want any issues selling the house.

Our luck seemed to be going OK, in fact the house sold in record timing! However, a week later my husband lost his job. He had never been fired in his life! Could it have been the construction in the West?

I quickly realized that I had completely overlooked one key factor. My husband's desk had been positioned towards the West for the past three months. Facing the Duke for hours at a time could have serious consequences. This factor, combined with the house construction, turned out to be detrimental.

Immediately upon realizing this, my husband humored me and my feng shui theory. We repositioned the desk so that he was no longer facing the Grand Duke. In less than a month, he had gotten another job offer with even better benefits.

Whether or not you believe in the superstitions of the Grand Duke Jupiter, it pays to know where he is! If your year is not going so well, make sure you are not facing him for extended periods of time. Consider changing the direction in which you sleep, watch TV, or work and it could turn your luck around quickly!

How to Avoid Mishaps with the Grand Duke Jupiter
1. Try not to sit facing, or sleep with your head pointing to, the direction of Grand Duke Jupiter.
2. Avoid construction work including repair work, in the Tai Sui location. The Grand Duke Jupiter dislikes noise and commotion.
3. Appease the Grand Duke by placing his pet, the Pi Yao, in the affected sector. For example, if the Duke is in the West for the year, face Pi Yao towards the West.

Figure 17.1

Calculate your Best Direction:

Now it is time to discover your four personal best directions. Here is how! Take the last two numbers of the year you were born and add them together. Reduce them down to a single digit. For example, if you were born in 1957 then you take the **57**.

$$5+7=12$$
$$1+2=3$$

If you are male subtract the last number from 10. If you are female add 5 to your number.

MALE – take the single digit and subtract it from 10. Example: 1957 single number of 3; 10-3=7. The Kua number is 7.

FEMALE – take the single digit and add 5. Using the 1957 single number of 3; 3+5=8. The Kua number is 8.

Teaching from the Heart with Feng Shui

Kua Number	Success (Sheng Chi)	Health (Tien Yi)	Relationships (Nien Yen)	Personal Development (Fu Wei)
1	SE	E	S	N
2	NE	W	NW	SW
3	S	N	SE	E
4	N	S	E	SE
5 (Male)	NE	W	NW	SW
5 (Female)	SW	NW	W	NE
6	W	NE	SW	NW
7	NW	SW	NE	W
8	SW	NW	W	NE
9	E	SE	N	S

Figure 17.2

Once you know your "best direction," you should sit towards it for optimal results. You can download a free compass application on your phone to see which direction you are facing. I have actually used the "best direction" formula to determine which seat is best for my family members and I at the dining room table. When I took an online exam, I used my best direction for personal success to help me determine where to sit. These are just a few examples of how you could use this to attract greater inner-peace and prosperity.

> **Remember...**
>
> Even when you face your best direction, it is still ideal to have a "mountain behind you." When you have a solid wall behind you, you will feel more secure. It is also most auspicious to see the entrance of the room when you are seated. This makes you feel more at ease because subconsciously you know that no one will be "sneaking up on you."

Your Turn!

Try Activity 7 in the Appendix, "All About You." It serves as a clear guide to finding your best directions. It also provides a reflective component so that you can brainstorm ways in which you can use your personal best directions to your advantage!

Chapter 18
Attracting Abundance with Transcendental Cures

"You have to believe it before you can see it."
-Dr. Wayne Dyer

Feng shui is a combination of mundane and transcendental cures. The mundane aspects of feng shui are the visible changes that you make to your home or classroom, such as rearranging furniture or hanging a mirror. These adjustments are more logical and apparent. They are easy to understand, and easily accepted by intellectuals.

Transcendental adjustments are called chu-shr in Chinese, meaning "outside our experience," and they go beyond our understanding. These cures may seem illogical or superstitious, but their purpose is to connect us with the heavenly realms. Meditations and blessings are examples of transcendental cures, and when combined with the mundane, this is a powerful connection of feng shui.

Using sage to release the energy in a room, or wind chimes to circulate the chi, are both transcendental cures. Feng shui practitioners can perform a "Sealing of the Toilet" adjustment in order to prevent energy from leaking down the drains. These invisible cures are difficult to understand, but they have been proven effective time and again since feng shui originated over 3,000 years ago.

Both types of adjustments are important to utilize in order to achieve optimal results. If you want your environment to look *and* feel good you must take both into consideration. This chapter gives you yet another way to look at the bagua map in order to apply transcendental cures.

Attracting Wealth with Transcendental Cures

Transcendental adjustments are mostly symbolic and may seem strange. They can be great to perform in spaces such as your garage or crawl space, since no one really sees those areas. My garage occupies the knowledge, family and wealth guas. I do not like to spend much time there, but I have made it a point to place artifacts in each gua of the garage so that those areas are being enhanced.

In the wealth area of the garage, I have placed eight purple envelopes with one dollar in each. Purple activates the wealth gua, and eight symbolizes infinite abundance in feng shui. Behind the envelopes, I have placed a mirror to "multiply" the wealth. (Mirrors duplicate anything they reflect, so make sure you are reflecting more of what you wish to attract!)

After placing the envelopes in the wealth gua, I said a prayer or blessing to seal my intention. I continually clear out that space in the garage to keep the energy and abundance flowing in.

There are many cures that you can apply to your home to attract more wealth! The number "4" represents the wealth gua as well as "8." As you familiarize yourself with the different adjustments, you can get creative with how you apply them.

Wealth Adjustments

Write the number 88 (double your money number) in a desk drawer or somewhere you see it every day.
Place a mirror under a bowl of fruit on the dining room table.
Place 9 $100 dollar bills in separate red envelopes under the mattress. This is faster than any other adjustment according to Professor Thomas Lin Yun. If you do not have 9 $100 dollar bills, use 9 of the same increments (i.e. 9 $5 dollar bills or 9 $20 bills).

Avoid leaving your wallet exposed (such as on the counter). Keep it in your bedroom or somewhere out of sight.
Place your purse on the table rather than the floor. Carry it in gratitude, and treat it with respect since it is the carrier of your abundance.
Carry three Chinese coins tied with red ribbon in your purse or wallet.

Figure 18.1

Once you apply some of the wealth adjustments, look out for the signs! Abundance comes to us in many different forms, not just money. Maybe someone will bring you an unexpected cup of coffee or go out of their way to help you with something. Pay attention to the signs that the universe is listening to your call for help, and notice all the ways that it is supporting you. The more you recognize these simple gestures and see them as gifts, the more grateful you will feel. And the more grateful you are, the more you will have to be grateful for!

There are many wealth adjustments sprinkled throughout the book. The next section will also give more ideas on how to attract abundance in all areas of your life. Remember that the key is always to keep it simple and have fun!

More Invisible Cures for Each Gua

The Symbolism of Numbers Chart (Figure 18.2) provides the number associated with each gua. The numbers can be used to activate each area.

The relationship gua is enhanced by the number two. If you are looking to attract a partner or improve your current relationship, placing pairs of objects (of similar size to promote equality) can help you activate that part of your life. The suggestions provided in the table are simply ideas. You can use the knowledge of each gua to personalize it and make it work for you and your environment.

The Symbolism of Numbers

Gua/Area of Life	Number Association	What the Number Represents	A Trick to Enhance This Area of Life
Career	1	1 is the number for new beginnings and independence. Living in a "1" house is great for independent entrepreneurs who are starting a business.	On a single piece of paper, write a positive affirmation of what you wish for your career. Place the affirmation behind a mirror or painting in the career area and say a blessing. No one will see it, but you will know it is there and your intentions will be heard.
Relationship	2	2 symbolizes partnership, learning to compromise, and teamwork. When you live in a "2" house you will learn how cooperate with your loved ones and expand.	Add two swallow birds or candles to the relationship area. Place the objects close to each other. If you put pairs of objects far apart, it could have the opposite result on your relationship. In a classroom, place two chairs (or any even number of chairs) in this area to promote collaboration among students, teachers, and staff.

Family	3	3 is the number of stability, the balance of energy, the circle of energy, and harmony. Living in a "3" home will feel satisfying.	Add three picture frames with recent, happy family photos in the family gua. Also, consider paying bills in this space because it represents always having enough to support the family.
Wealth	4	4 represents wealth and security. However, a "4" house in feng shui is considered undesirable. "4" in Chinese sounds like the word "death." It is recommended to get a consultant to energetically change the number.	Place four or eight quarters or silver dollars in a flower pot (by the front entrance), or in a bonsai or money tree in your wealth area. Say a prayer or blessing to increase your abundance.
Health	5	5 is the number of health, creativity, and balance. 5 is in the middle of 1-9 so it is considered neutral. Living in a "5" house promotes creative expression.	Write five positive affirmations for your health on 5 different yellow post-it notes (yellow squares represent Earth). Place the sticky notes behind a frame or artwork. No one will see this but you will know it is there and your intentions will be heard.

Helpful People/Travel	6	The number 6 is the number to activate spiritual guides in feng shui, but numerology generally associates 7 with this. A "6" house is a great place to raise a family. It is very nurturing.	Place a silver, gold, or bronze colored dish or container in the helpful people area. Place coins in the jar. Use the money to donate to a charity that is dear to you. "When you always give, you'll always have" (Chinese Proverb). What you give always comes back to you.
Children/ Creativity	7	7 is a spiritual number. If you live in a "7" house, you will connect with your Higher Self.	This area is represented and activated by lakes. You could add a picture of a lake in this area and put 7 affirmations on the back of it for what your wishes are for your children. Use this space to work on creative projects such as writing, crafts, or curriculum planning.

Wisdom/ Knowledge	8	8 is the infinity sign. It represents wealth and abundance. If you live in an "8" house, you will have great potential to build your wealth, as long as you keep a positive mindset about money.	Money is energy. Just as you must inhale and exhale to breathe, you must learn to receive as well as give. That which you give, always comes back to you. Place 8 red or purple envelopes in the wealth area of your home. Fill each envelope with the same amount of money and say a prayer or blessing for more abundance.
Fame/ Reputation	9	9 is the most powerful and energetic number in feng shui. It is considered lucky. If you live in a "9" house, it is considered a stable place to reside.	Place nine quarters under a rug at the entrance of your home. Align the quarters in an arrow facing towards the house to welcome abundance in the house. Make sure the coins connect so that the energy is more powerful. Always say a blessing or affirmation after making an adjustment such as this.

Figure 18.2 The house number representations are interpreted based on the principles of feng shui and numerology.

The Significance of Even or Odd Numbers

If you are activating a gua, but the number does not suit your decor, here is a great tip to give you more flexibility; if a gua is activated by an even number, you can generally use any even number, or visa-versa.

Let's say you want to improve the way you are seen by your employers, clients, family and/or friends. You would want to enhance the Fame and Reputation gua; this area is activated by the number nine and the fire element. You might feel inclined to light a candle in this space, but nine candles might be excessive. Since nine is an odd number, you could light one or three candles with the intention of improving your reputation. This would be particularly beneficial to do if you are getting ready for a job interview.

Getting Creative with Feng Shui

As you can see, feng shui is very versatile. It is often open to interpretation, which allows you to get creative with your applications. Feng shui is meant to be flexible and fun. Use the tips and tools that you learned in this chapter to get the results you want. Add your own unique style, and let your creativity guide you into the life you desire.

Try Activity 8 in the Appendix, "Fun with Feng Shui Numbers." This activity will give you a chance to think about how to activate all the guas in your home using the magical transcendental cures suggested throughout this chapter. Although no one will see these feng shui adjustments, you will set new intentions and feel the difference for yourself!

Chapter 19
Finding Balance by Aligning with Nature

"Thank you Universe for all the good things in my life that I don't yet know about."
-Abraham Hicks

Many people start their feng shui journey because they want their home or office to look and feel better. Once they start to learn more about it, they realize that it is a tool of self-empowerment; one that will help you change and improve your life in so many ways. Once you are aware that everything around you has energy, you are more conscious of everything you do.

One way to heighten your feng shui awareness is by paying attention to the cycles of our planet and the universe. These cycles affect everyone collectively, so their impacts can be major. Knowing the cycles of the moon and the effects of the change in season can give you deeper self-awareness and more compassion towards others. When you become aware of the natural energies around you, you learn to embrace them and use them to your advantage.

For example, the New Moon can leave you feeling very tired and drained. It is not an ideal time to start a new project or take action during this time. Rather, the New Moon is a good time to go within and set your intention for what you wish to accomplish and attract into your life. Knowing these cycles can help you follow the natural flow of life instead of paddling upstream, going against the current.

Nature's Cycles

Cycle	How to Go with the Flow
New Moon	The New Moon appears to be completely dark and unseen. The darkness is quiet, yin energy. Use this time to go within; meditate or write down some of your wishes for the upcoming month. Do not take action yet. Any obstacles that may be holding you back will reveal themselves to you by the next Full Moon.
Full Moon	The Full Moon is when the moon appears at its largest. The bright light emitted is yang, or active energy. Although this energy can actually make you feel tired or overwhelmed, if embraced and redirected, the energy of the Full Moon is a great time to be productive and complete unfinished projects.
Mercury Retrograde	Several times a year Mercury appears to rotate reversely. Since this planet rules communication, it is good to know when Mercury is in Retrograde because it will most likely affect your technology (e-mails, cell phone connections, etc.) and travel. During this time, it is best to avoid making any large purchases, especially homes, cars, or electronics. It is a good time to revise, edit, and complete unfinished projects.
New Year	Every New Year is a chance to set a new tone for the year ahead. Feng shui has many recommendations for starting the year fresh, and there are many ways to open up the opportunities of abundance in the upcoming year. It is a great time to conduct an Orange Peel Blessing, open all the windows to let in fresh chi, and welcome in the Wealth Gods for the year. I started these traditions in my home last New Year, and it was the best year yet!

The Four Seasons	All four seasons have unique qualities and are represented by different elements. If you become familiar with the natural flow and tendencies of each season, you can embrace the cycles instead of going against them. **Summer:** (Ruled by fire element) Embrace the electric fire energy and be active over the summer. It is a great time to improve your fame and reputation. **Fall:** (Activated by Earth element) The fall is a time when we become more grounded. Although it is less whimsical than summer, you can still keep the momentum going in the fall, but give yourself time to rest so you don't get overworked. **Winter:** (Represented by water element) Go with the flow during this "cool" time. Stay persistent with projects so they are ready to blossom in the spring. **Spring:** (Enhanced by wood element) Exercise your flexibility during the springtime. Be open to the new ideas of others and collaborate.

Figure 19.1

Chapter 20
Finding Balance Within

"One conscious breath-in and out- is a meditation."
-Eckhart Tolle

Just as you can use nature's cycles to help you go with the flow of universal energy, you can become more aware of your body's natural rhythms and improve your personal energy.

One way to keep your mind and body in balance is by becoming mindful of your chakras. The seven chakras align with the center of your body along the spine. Each chakra represents a significant aspect of our being. When a chakra is blocked, it could cause stress or illness.

You can align your chakras by consciously focusing on each one. Saying the positive affirmations and taking deep breaths throughout the day can also help you stay centered, focused, and more relaxed.

The Balancing Your Chakras chart (Figure 20.1) explains the significance of each chakra. It provides suggested affirmations that you can say to clear them. Since chakras are associated with particular colors, the chart suggests different stones and crystals in nature that could be used to enhance each chakra.

Balancing Your Chakras

Chakra & Color	Representation	Positive Affirmation to Heal the Chakra	Stone
Root Chakra- Red	Represents our foundation and feelings of financial security, that all our needs are met	I am perfectly protected in all ways and all of my needs are met and provided for at every moment.	Red tigers eye or garnet
Sacral Chakra- Orange	Our ability to accept others and new experiences	All of my desires are perfectly balanced.	Orange calcite
Solar Plexus- Yellow	Our ability to be confident and in control of our lives	I release any fears or struggles concerning my power and control. I have perfect power and control. This power has pure motivation to love and serve all of life. I create a beautiful, harmonious day.	Citrine
Heart Chakra- Green	Our ability to love and heal	I am willing to release any fears of giving and receiving love.	Jade or rose quartz
Throat Chakra- Blue	Our ability to communicate	I willingly release all fear that would keep me from speaking my truth today. I allow my Higher Self and Holy Spirit to speak through me today. Today everyone I come in contact with benefits from listening to my words.	Lapis

Third Eye Chakra- Purple	Awareness and our ability to see the big picture	I am willing to release all fears of seeing the truth. I am safe as I allow my Higher Self to see the truth.	Amethyst (dark)
Crown Chakra- Purple/ White	Our ability to be fully connected spiritually	I release all fear about listening to my Higher Self, God, and Angels. I know that I am perfectly safe as I follow my inner spiritual guidance. I allow this guidance to lead me to new opportunities where I am seen for my true, beautiful nature. I listen, I trust, and I take guided action.	Clear quartz or amethyst (light)

Figure 20.1 Affirmations quoted from Doreen Virtue, Ph.D. *Chakra Clearing App*, Oceanhouse Media (2010).

Daily Chakra Healing

Balancing your chakras will help you heal wounds from the past so that you can have a more positive outlook and grow into a lighter, more authentic version of yourself. Intentional breathing and shifting your thoughts towards positive self-talk are the first steps toward changing your reality and feeling greater inner peace.

Chapter 21
Finding Your Flow

"If you can dream it, you can do it."
-Walt Disney

What is the Feng Shui Flow?

When you are in the flow with feng shui, your inner world and outer worlds are cohesive. Things feel as good as they look, and they look as good as they feel. When something feels off or you are experiencing a challenge in your life, you know that you are empowered to change it with simple feng shui cures or adjustments.

Sometimes all you need to do is rearrange some picture frames or move a plant to a new location in order to get the chi circulating and welcome a new perspective into your life. Cleaning and making slight changes to your physical can be exactly what you need to feel better.

While organizing, decorating, and rearranging furniture can get things moving, it is just as important to address the invisible, transcendental aspects of feng shui. You may want to use Sage Spray throughout the day to clear any negative or stressful energy. You could carry a crystal around with you to protect you from other people's chi so that you do not feel drained. Most importantly, you need to find some sacred time every day to center yourself.

On Your Way with Feng Shui

You will start to see and feel profound results as you incorporate feng shui in your day-to-day life. Now that you know the basics, you can start to embrace the feng shui principles and make them your own.

Since your life is always changing, you will always have a need to use feng shui. Once you feng shui a bedroom or office, it is never finished. You will find yourself checking in on your spaces more regularly, especially since you are more aware of the effect that your objects and surroundings have on the flow of all aspects of your life.

Do not fret; keeping up with the feng shui of your home, office, or classroom will not feel like a chore. As you clean, rearrange, and re-energize your space on a regular basis, you will feel the difference almost immediately. These instant results make feng shui rewarding.

Namaste

If I could leave you will one final piece of advice, it would be to live in the now. Whatever your greatest dreams are, whatever your heart yearns for, think of one action step you can take today, and go for it.

When I started my feng shui journey, I just wanted my apartment to look and feel better. I had no idea that feng shui could actually help me to see my life with more clarity. It connected me to new, helpful people and opened up my eyes to fresh opportunities. Because of feng shui I can honestly say that I have become more of my authentic self, and that is the true key to happiness.

If I would have waited to get my feng shui certification, or waited to write this book, it may not have ever happened. I seized the opportunities as they came to me. Whatever your dreams are, don't be afraid to take the first step. Once you do, the next step will become clear to you.

As we go through this journey of life, we all have lessons to learn. There will be challenges and times of pain. Feng shui cannot change that. However, feng shui is a tool that can help you through all of life's seasons. Although I still experience struggles, I have a new perspective on which to deal with them. I feel empowered to make changes so that all of life's speed bumps can be used for good.

Don't wait for a better time to do something that is on your heart. Maybe you have a hobby that you've neglected. That is your gift. Make time for it! You never know where it will take you. Maybe you want to expand your family, move to a new location, or start a new career. Take one step today. Your dreams and desires are divinely given, specifically for you. You were meant to fulfill your dreams. Start living them today with the help of feng shui.

Nine Do-It-Yourself Feng Shui Activities!

Table of Contents:

1. The Nine Areas of Life: Using the Bagua Map *(Chapter 1)*

2. Let's Get Energized: Understanding the Flow of Chi *(Chapter 2)*

3. Improve Your Life with the Elements: Introduction to the Five Elements *(Chapters 3, 7, and 16)*

4. All About Affirmations *(Chapters 4 and 8)*

5. Let's Find More Balance: Yin & Yang *(Chapters 1 and 6)*

6. Feng Shui Your Bedroom *(Chapters 11 and 14)*

7. All About You: Finding Your Best Direction *(Chapter 17)*

8. Fun with Feng Shui Numbers *(Chapter 18)*

9. Living the Feng Shui Way: Evaluate Your Personal Chi *(Chapter 21)*

How to Use These Activities

The nine activities will help you apply the feng shui concepts to your home and classroom with greater ease and clarity. Each exercise is best matched to specific chapters of the book. The chapters in which the activities correlate with are written in parentheses in the Table of Contents, but they can be practiced at any time, in any order.

These activities are for teachers, parents, students and all learners of feng shui. They are designed to help you reflect on the lessons taught throughout the book and start a personalized plan to implement feng shui immediately.

Once you try them for yourself, share the feng shui strategies with children at your leisure. The activities will provide kids with a foundation to become more aware of their surroundings and take ownership of their environment. Regardless of how the activities are used, they will empower children and adults alike.

Activity 1

The Nine Areas of Life

What is the bagua map? Feng shui is the ancient Chinese practice of organizing and decorating your space to create internal and external harmony. The bagua map is a tool that you can use to help you improve all nine areas of your life. When you lay the map on the floor plan of your classroom, bedroom, or entire house, you can see which rooms or sections correlate with the specific gua of life.

Directions:

1. Draw a picture of your house, classroom, bedroom. Try to draw it as close to scale as possible.

2. Grab a ruler, pencil, and a calculator. Divide the room into nine equal squares.

3. Label your sketch. The front door will either be in the wisdom & knowledge, career, or helpful people & travel guas.

4. After you label each gua, color the gua with an activating color.

5. Finally, draw a picture of the shape in each gua that will activate the space.

Wall That Contains the Main Entrance (Front Door)

Activity 2

Let's Get Energized!

What is Chi? The flow of chi is all around you. Chi, or energy, is the invisible life force according to the ancient Chinese practice of feng shui. When energy flows uninterrupted, it rejuvenates us and makes us feel more alert, peaceful, and confident. Chi enters through the classroom door. Although chi is invisible air, imagine that it is a river. Imagine where the water flows as it enters your classroom. Does the water get stuck somewhere? Does the water get piled up in a certain spot? Your job is to find out how the chi flows through your classroom. After you try this with your classroom, you can do the same activity sketching your bedroom or other rooms in your house. Happy feng shui-ing!

Directions:

1. Draw your classroom (include the door, windows, desks, and big furniture pieces).

2. With a crayon, trace the flow of "water" from the front door. DO NOT lift up your crayon. See where the water can flow. Does it stop somewhere? Is there a place in the room where the "water" cannot reach?

3. Draw a new sketch of your classroom. See if you can arrange the furniture so that the water can flow everywhere in the room.

Activity 3

Improve Your Life with the Elements

What are the elements? According to feng shui there are five different elements: water, fire, wood, metal, and earth. You can represent the elements with shape and color. It is best to place the elements in the coordinating gua.

Decor Suggestions to Represent Each Element:

1. **Earth:** square or rectangular (horizontal) picture frames, yellow throw blanket or accent pillows, sand colored towels, sand or rocks in a square dish, a salt lamp, fresh flowers or silk flowers that look real

2. **Water:** picture of the ocean, fish tank, water fountain, thunderstorm or ocean sounds, mirrors

3. **Fire:** candles, fireplace, picture with reds or bright orange, triangular patterns, fur, leather, feathers

4. **Wood:** rectangular frames (vertical), wooden sculptures or dishes, wood furniture, bamboo plant, money tree, bonsai tree

5. **Metal:** metal dishes, circular frames or clocks, metallic artwork, gray or white throw pillows or curtains

1. Knowledge is represented by the Earth element. Looking at the chart, what kind of decorations could you add to the knowledge gua to increase your wisdom and clarity? _____
_____
_____
_____

2. Wealth is represented by the wood element. This is a great space to activate if you need more money or an abundance of time or resources. What kind of decor could you use to enhance your wealth? _____
_____
_____
_____

3. The fame and reputation gua is activated by fire. This is an appropriate area to enhance if you want people to see you in a positive light. How could you decorate this area to improve how you are viewed by the world? _____
_____
_____
_____

Activity 3 (Continued)

The Five Elements

1. **Earth: square: yellow, sand colors, beige**

2. **Water: odd shapes (waves): blues and black**

3. **Fire: triangle: red, orange, yellow**

4. **Wood: rectangle (vertical/up and down): browns and greens**

5. **Metal: circle: grey and white**

Table One: First, focus on shape. Look around your classroom at some of the student work, posters, and other decorations. You can even notice the shape of the furniture. Which element do these objects represent?

Object	Shape	Element

Table Two: Next, focus on color. Look around your classroom again. Notice the color of the decorations and furniture. Which element do these objects represent?

Object	Shape	Element

Which objects could be moved so that they are activating a gua, or area of life? _____
_____
_____
_____

*Extension: Try this at home on your bedroom! What elements are represented there? Do you have a mirror, picture frames or candles that could be moved to a more appropriate gua? Remember to have fun, and think about what you want to attract into your life as you decorate. Positive changes are coming your way!

Activity 4

All About Affirmations

What is an affirmation? Affirmations are words that you think or say, and believe to be true. You can affirm positive or negative things about yourself and your life. The choice is yours! Many of our thoughts become our reality, so why not try to create a life that makes us feel happy and peaceful within? Louise Hay and Kristina Tracy (2008) who wrote *I Think, I Am!* suggests several tips for doing affirmations such as:

1. Always start an affirmation with positive words such as: *I can, I am, I do, I have.*

2. Say your affirmation over and over, whenever you think of it.

3. Say an affirmation especially when you are having a lot of unhappy/negative thoughts.

4. Write down your affirmations in a notebook or journal.

5. Close your eyes and picture what you want -- this is an affirmation.

Directions: Review some of the negative affirmations. In the chart below, change the negative thoughts into positive ones. The more you practice this skill, the better you will feel.

Negative Affirmations	Positive Affirmation
Everyone is leaving me out... No one likes me...	
I always make mistakes... Why can't I do anything right?	
My toys (or clothes or other material items) are never as nice as hers...	
I never get to do what I want...	

Can you think of other negative affirmations you have been telling yourself? Write some of the negative things you think or say. Then, try to turn those statements into positive ones.

My old thoughts/words	My new thoughts/words

Activity 5

Let's Find More Balance!

What are yin and yang? All objects have either yin or yang characteristics. **Yin** is passive. It symbolizes darkness, stillness, quietness, and flexibility. **Yang** is active. It symbolizes light, activity, movement, and strength. It is important to have both of these elements in a room, but some rooms need more yin, while others need more yang. For example, your bedroom should have more yin so that you can relax and feel restful. While a basement or playroom could have more yang energy so that people feel energized in the space while they are socializing.

Directions: Look at the chart below. It explains how to represent yin and yang in each space. Then, make a list of objects in your classroom (or bedroom). Place the objects in the column.

How to Represent Yin	How to Represent Yang
• Dim lights • Colors: white, pastels, gray • Solid colors, soft textures (fur) • Furniture with rounded edges • Classical music • Candles • Sheer curtains • Soft pillows	• Bright lights • Colors: red, bright colors • Patterns, rough textures • Furniture with pointed edges • Electronics (TVs, computers, SMART boards) • Upbeat music • Plants

My Room

Objects in my room	Yin or Yang?

1. Do you have more yin or yang represented? _____

2. What could you add or remove to balance the space? __
   _____
   _____

Activity 6

Feng Shui Your Bedroom

About the Bedroom: You spend about a third of your life sleeping. Therefore, you spend about a third of your life in your bedroom. Just as you plug in your cell phone to charge it, when you sleep your body is "recharging." In order to wake up feeling refreshed, you need to try to place your bed in the **power position**.

How to put your bed in the Power Position:

1. **Arrange your bed against a solid wall with your feet facing the door, but not in line with it.** When your head is to a solid wall, it creates a "mountain behind you." The mountain behind you makes you feel secure. Just as importantly, you want to be able to see the door. This gives you greater peace of mind knowing that no one will sneak into your room without you noticing. If you cannot put your head against a solid wall, draw the curtains when you sleep at night.

2. **Be able to access the bed from both sides.** You do not want to put the bed against the wall. Imagine that the energy circles around you as you sleep. The energy flows above your head, and then it circles down underneath your bed and back up again. Around it goes. If you are against the wall, the energy gets stuck, and you will feel less rested. Additionally, it could keep you from getting into a relationship when you are ready to start dating!

3. **Don't keep anything under your bed.** Clear the clutter from underneath your bed. The energy needs to circulate around you when you sleep so that you feel rested.

The Bagua Map: You can use a tool called a bagua map to improve nine areas of your life (fame, career, wealth, relationships, health, creativity, family, travel, and knowledge). When you lay the bagua map on the floor plan of your bedroom, you can find out which area of your room correlates to certain areas of your life.

Wealth	Fame and Reputation	Relationship
Colors: Purple, Green, Gold	Colors: Red	Colors: Pink, Skin tones
Family	**Health Center**	**Children and Creativity**
Colors: Green, Brown	Colors: Yellow, Earth tones	Colors: White, Bright, Pastel
Wisdom and Self Knowledge	**Career**	**Helpful People and Travel**
Colors: Blue-green	Colors: Dark Blue, Black	Colors: Gray, Mauve

Wall that contains the main entrance

Activity 6 (Continued)

Directions: Sketch a picture of your bedroom. Label the major furniture pieces, the windows and doors. Is there any way you could rearrange your furniture so that the bed is in the power position? Next, lay the bagua map on your bedroom sketch. Which areas of your room could you start to declutter first? Which area of your life will improve after you declutter, clean, and perhaps decorate?

Activity 7

All About You!

About Personal Direction: Everyone has four "Best Directions". You have a best direction for success, health, relationships, and personal development. When you are aware of this information, you can use it to your advantage. You can download a compass app onto your phone so that you can sit in your best directions anywhere, at any time!

Face in the direction of **success** when you are looking to have a successful conversation with someone. Perhaps you are asking your parents for something that you really want to do. Facing the success direction will give you more ideas to help you be more prosperous. Sit towards the **health** direction as often as you like, especially if you are fighting a cold. You may want to sit in the **relationship** direction at the lunch or dinner table. This will help you have better interactions with friends and family. Turn towards the **personal development** direction when you are learning something new. This would be a great direction to face when doing homework or taking a test.

Directions: Find out your personal direction using the chart below. Then, answer the reflection questions.

Calculate your Best Direction:

Take the last two numbers of the year you were born and add them together. Reduce them down to a single digit. For example, if you were born in 1957 then you take the 57; 5+7=12; 1+2=3.

If you are male subtract the last number from 10.

If you are female add 5 to your number.

MALE – take the single digit and subtract it from 10. Example: 1957 single number of 3; 10-3=7. The Kua number is 7.

FEMALE – take the single digit and add 5. Using the 1957 single number of 3; 3+5=8. The Kua number is 8.

Activity 7 (Continued)

Kua Number	Success (Sheng Chi)	Health (Tien Yi)	Relationships (Nien Yen)	Personal Development (Fu Wei)
1	SE	E	S	N
2	NE	W	NW	SW
3	S	N	SE	E
4	N	S	E	SE
5 (Male)	NE	W	NW	SW
5 (Female)	SW	NW	W	NE
6	W	NE	SW	NW
7	NW	SW	NE	W
8	SW	NW	W	NE
9	E	SE	N	S

1. My best direction for success is _____. I may want to face this direction when _____.

2. My best direction for health is _____. I may want to face this direction when _____.

3. My best direction for relationships is _____. I may want to face this direction when _____.

4. My best direction for personal development is _____. I may want to face this direction when _____.

Activity 8

Fun with Feng Shui Numbers!

Why are numbers significant in feng shui? Numbers 1-9 have a special meaning in feng shui. You can use this knowledge to help you enhance any area of your life. When you are decorating your room or classroom, you can use the numbers in order to activate the space so that it feels more tranquil.

Directions:

1. Place the bagua map on the floor plan of your bedroom or classroom.
2. Notice where each gua is located in the room.
3. Which number activates the space? Use the examples for each gua to give you ideas.

Bagua Map

Wealth Element: wood Shape: vertical rectangle Colors: green, gold, purple *Number: 4*	Fame/Reputation Element: fire Shape: triangle Colors: Red, bright orange *Number: 9*	Relationship Element: Earth Shape: square or horizontal rectangle Colors: pink, skin tones, Earth tones *Number: 2*
Family Element: wood Shape: vertical rectangle Colors: green, brown *Number: 3*	Health Element: Earth Shape: square or horizontal rectangle Colors: Yellow, Earth tones *Number: 5*	Children/Creativity Element: metal Shape: circle Colors: white, pastel colors, gray *Number: 7*
Knowledge Element: Earth Shape: square or horizontal rectangle Colors: blue, green, earth tones *Number: 8*	Career Element: water Shape: wavy/odd Colors: blue, black or mirrors to represent water *Number: 1*	Helpful People/Travel Element: metal Shape: circle Colors: white, pastel colors, gray *Number: 6*

Activity 8 (Continued)

Activity: How can you use the numbers of the bagua map to activate the different areas of your bedroom, classroom, or house? Each area represents a different area of your life. When you enhance your environment, you will feel improvements in your life. Complete each sentence below to brainstorm how numbers can help you improve your space.

1. Number one is in the _____gua. I could enhance this gua with one _____
   _____.

2. Number two is in the _____gua. I could enhance this gua with two _____
   _____.

3. Number three is in the _____gua. I could enhance this gua with three _____
   _____.

4. Number four is in the _____gua. I could enhance this gua with four _____
   _____.

5. Number five is in the _____gua. I could enhance this gua with five _____
   _____.

6. Number six is in the _____gua. I could enhance this gua with six _____
   _____.

7. Number seven is in the _____gua. I could enhance this gua with seven_____
   _____.

8. Number eight is in the _____ gua. I could enhance this gua with eight _____.

9. Number nine is in the _____ gua. I could enhance this gua with nine _____.

*If you do not want to use the number of objects listed, you could use an even amount for all the even guas (2, 4, 6, and 8) and odd amounts for all the odd guas (1,3,5,7, and 9).

Activity 9

Living the Feng Shui Way: Evaluate Your Personal Chi

What is your *personal chi*? Your personal chi is your personal energy and how you feel throughout day. Each moment you have the power to make little choices that add up to one BIG picture! The music you listen to, the television shows you watch, and the books you read all make a difference on your personal energy and well-being. Let's take an inventory of some of your favorite pastimes and take the time to think about how they make you feel.

My Choices
My favorite music and songs are…
The shows I watch on TV are…
The magazines or internet articles I read are…
In my spare time I enjoy…
The people I spend the most time with are…

Reflection: Look at your personal choices. Think about how you feel when you listen to certain music. Do you engage in gossip or play violent video games? How do you feel when you watch the news?

What you feed your mind affects how you feel. The people you surround yourself with can inspire and support you, or they can make you feel insecure and hide your authentic light. You do not have to change everything about your life choices right now, but being aware of the effect that everything has on you is the first step towards a happier, more fulfilling life.

Prompt: What are some alternative musicians, shows, or books that will make you feel uplifted and better about yourself? When you feel like the best version of yourself, who are you spending time with? This reflection is meant to EMPOWER you. You have the ability to change your life and feel better with every choice you make.

References

Anderson, J.C. (2010). *The de-cluttered school: How to create a cleaner, calmer, and greener learning Environment.* New York, NY: Continuum International Publishing Group.

Bloom, D. (2016). *Instead of detention, these students get meditation.* Retrieved from www.cnn.com/2016/11/04/health/meditation-in-schools-baltimore/index.html

Claudat, D. (2013). *Feng Shui 101: A guide to finding your flow of fabulous.* United States of America: Dana Shui LLC

Danielson, C. (2007). *Enhancing professional practice: A framework for teaching. 2nd Ed.* Alexandria, VA: ASCD.

Davidji (2012). *Secrets of meditation: A practical guide to inner peace and personal transformation.* United States: Hay House Inc.

Dyer, W.W. and Tracy, K. (2006). *Unstoppable Me: 10 Ways to soar through life.* Carlsbad, CA: Hay House, Inc.

Editor, Y. (2016). *Meet darnell mcdonald, mental skills coordinator for the chicago cubs.* Retrieved from yogajournallive.com

Grace, C. (2013). *Feng Shui Simply: Change your life from the inside out.* Carlsbad, CA: Hay House, Inc.

Grout, P. (2013). *E-Squared: Nine do-it-yourself energy experiments that prove your thoughts create your reality.* Carlsbad, CA: Hay House, Inc.

Hay, L. and Tracy. K. (2008). *I think, I am: Teaching kids the power of affirmations.* Carlsbad, CA: Hay House, Inc.

Heiss, R. (2004). *Feng shui for the classroom:101 Easy-to-use-ideas.* Chicago, IL: Zephyr Press.

Mackail, D. (2016). *Feng Shui: Create health, wealth, and happiness through the power of Your home.* Carlsbad, CA: Hay House, Inc.

Morsella, E., Larson, L., Pareezad, Z. and Bargh, J. (2011). *Stimulus control: The sought or unsought influence of the objects we tend to.* Psicologica, *Vol. 32*, 145-169.

Rose, A. (2016). *Classroom feng shui.* Retrieved from cleburnetimesreview.com/news/classroom-feng-shui/article

Virtue, D. (1997). *Chakra clearing (audio).* Hay House Inc. & Oceanhouse Media Inc.

Made in the USA
Las Vegas, NV
23 May 2022